Audiovisual Translation in the Digital Age

DOI: 10.1057/9781137470379.0001

Other Palgrave Pivot titles

John Board, Alfonso Dufour, Yusuf Hartavi, Charles Sutcliffe and Stephen Wells: Risk and Trading on London's Alternative Investment Market: The Stock Market for Smaller and Growing Companies

Franklin G. Mixon, Jr: Public Choice Economics and the Salem Witchcraft Hysteria

Elisa Menicucci: Fair Value Accounting: Key Issues Arising from the Financial Crisis

Nicoletta Pireddu: The Works of Claudio Magris: Temporary Homes, Mobile Identities, European Borders

Larry Patriquin: Economic Equality and Direct Democracy in Ancient Athens

Antoine Pécoud: Depoliticising Migration: Global Governance and International Migration Narratives

Gerri Kimber: Katherine Mansfield and the Art of the Short Story: A Literary Modernist

C. Paul Hallwood and Thomas J. Miceli: Maritime Piracy and Its Control: An Economic Analysis

Letizia Guglielmo and Lynée Lewis Gaillet (editors): Contingent Faculty Publishing in Community: Case Studies for Successful Collaborations

Katie Digan: Places of Memory: The Case of the House of the Wannsee Conference

Mario La Torre: The Economics of the Audiovisual Industry: Financing TV, Film and Web

Piero Formica: The Role of Creative Ignorance: Portraits of Path Finders and Path Creators

James Carson: The Columbian Covenant: Race and the Writing of American History

Tomasz Kamusella: Creating Languages in Central Europe during the Last Millennium

Imad A. Moosa and Kelly Burns: Demystifying the Meese–Rogoff Puzzle

Kazuhiko Togo and GVC Naidu (editors): Building Confidence in East Asia: Maritime Conflicts, Interdependence and Asian Identity Thinking

Aylish Wood: Software, Animation and the Moving Image: What's in the Box?

Mo Jongryn (editor): MIKTA, Middle Powers, and New Dynamics of Global Governance: The G20's Evolving Agenda

Holly Jarman: The Politics of Trade and Tobacco Control

DOI: 10.1057/9781137470379.0001

palgrave▸**pivot**

Audiovisual Translation in the Digital Age: The Italian Fansubbing Phenomenon

Serenella Massidda
Università degli Studi di Sassari, Italy

palgrave
macmillan

DOI: 10.1057/9781137470379.0001

First published 2015 by
PALGRAVE MACMILLAN

Palgrave Macmillan in the UK is an imprint of Macmillan Publishers Limited, registered in England, company number 785998, of Houndmills, Basingstoke, Hampshire, RG21 6XS.

Palgrave Macmillan in the US is a division of St Martin's Press LLC, 175 Fifth Avenue, New York, NY 10010.

Palgrave Macmillan is the global academic imprint of the above companies and has companies and representatives throughout the world.

Palgrave® and Macmillan® are registered trademarks in the United States, the United Kingdom, Europe and other countries.

ISBN: 978–1–137–47038–6 EPUB
ISBN: 978–1–137–47037–9 PDF
ISBN: 978–1–137–47036–2 Hardback

A catalogue record for this book is available from the British Library.

A catalog record for this book is available from the Library of Congress.

www.palgrave.com/pivot

DOI: 10.1057/9781137470379

Contents

DOI: 10.1057/9781137470379.0001

List of Figures

List of Tables

DOI: 10.1057/9781137470379.0003

DOI: 10.1057/9781137470379.0003

palgrave▶**pivot**

www.palgrave.com/pivot

Introduction

Abstract: *A methodological overview of the multi-layered approach employed in the investigation of the theory and practices adopted by the Italian fansubbing communities is provided in this section. Much has been drawn from the systems theories related to translation, in particular from Toury's Descriptive Translation Studies (1995) and Chesterman's subsequent studies regarding norms (1997), with special reference to the notion of "expectancy norms". In addition, the different approaches pertinent to the ideologies under examination within the field of Translation Studies, including the dichotomy between "domestication" and "foreignisation" examined by Schleiermacher (1813), Lewis' "abusive fidelity" (1985), Venuti's concept of the translator's "visibility" (2008) and Nornes's "abusive subtitling" (1999) have all concurred to clarify the orientation adopted by the fansubbing communities for their translations.*

Massidda, Serenella. *Audiovisual Translation in the Digital Age: The Italian Fansubbing Phenomenon.* Basingstoke: Palgrave Macmillan, 2015. DOI: 10.1057/9781137470379.0004.

> "An expansion of crowd-sourced translation risks obscuring
> the essential, but already underappreciated distinction,
> between subtitling a movie and translating its words."
>
> (Paletta 2012)

The above quotation was chosen as a brief example illustrating the prevailing opinion concerning the fansubbing phenomenon worldwide. Both academics and professionals can be rest assured that we might agree with this statement to some extent. Yet, the purpose of this study is not to demonstrate the superior quality of fansubbing over subtitling, since the aim is to explore the origin and evolution of the amateur translator's practice and beliefs, with particular reference to the impact that this phenomenon has had on audiovisual translation methodologies in Italy.

The inspiration behind this research into amateur translation came long before the PhD career path became a viable option for me. At that time, I was enrolled in the MSc programme in Scientific, Technical and Medical Translation with Translation Technology at Imperial College London (ICL). When the time came to decide on a topic for my final dissertation, I immediately thought of fansubbing as the most attractive option, since it represented a new research field with considerable potential.

The fansubbing project had, in fact, started three years earlier in Italy: I had been following the movements of fansubbers from their inception, so that I was already familiar with their practices and methodologies, and considering my background as a teacher of English and a subtitler, they obviously exerted a strong fascination over me. Unfortunately, I was forced to focus on another topic as far as the master's dissertation was concerned, since I realised that a longer period of investigation was mandatory for a field of audiovisual translation which was largely unresearched till five years ago. In fact, four years ago, when the PhD research project started, the first and foremost difficulty encountered was the absence of a substantial review of literature on the subject matter. I, thus, embarked on a long journey in search of relevant material not only on the same field of study, but also on correlated areas of research that might be of use to the project. It was thus that I came into contact with Media Studies, to find that various academics had studied the phenomenon of fan translation from an angle other than linguistics, namely from the point of view of the fans. The discovery was enlightening since I came to realise that, in order to understand fansubbing

DOI: 10.1057/9781137470379.0004

thoroughly, I had to shift my perspective from the point of view of the researcher to the perspective of the fan. This is, then, the story of a PhD candidate who became a fansubber.

Initially, I approached ItaSA by emailing them in order to take the test as a would-be-fansubber. As a result, I was sent a link to a video, a file with time codes and a link to the subtitling software necessary for the process. When it was ready, I submitted my translation and had to wait a week before finding out I was selected by ItaSA as a junior translator. A tutor assisted me during the trial period in which I was to produce a certain number of translations for the community. The worst part at first was the mastering of a variety of subtitling software programs which required long hours of practice, and in that particular phase of my research I could not find enough time to explore these aspects. As a consequence, my contribution to the community lasted only a few months, and I decided to leave it because I was unable to perform as many translations as required from me.

After a year, during a visit to the department of Humanities (Imperial College London), I decided that it was about time to get in contact with the other fansubbing community: Subsfactory. Upon successful completion of the entry test for translators, I became a SIP.[1]

A helpful tutor introduced me to the community and a proficient "master syncher" taught me how to cue the subtitles using the customised software. The trial period was hard, as I spent long hours attempting to master the timing process using open source resources, certainly less user-friendly than the professional ones I was already accustomed to. Yet, after a couple of months I became a fully-fledged "master subber".

The community was pleasantly welcoming and I found myself at ease with them.

Once I was part of the fansubbing machine, I was able to grasp how the organisation operated from the inside, namely the motivation behind their work, their passion as fans, along with their desire to learn English and share the fruit of their work with fellow fans. I also discovered that the fansubbers at Subsfactory took their "job" very seriously, showing a profound respect for the hierarchy (the revisers and administrators of the site) and particularly for the responsibility associated with the fansubbing process. Admittedly, I started to develop a dual personality: the researcher on one hand, and the fansubber on the other. Retrospectively, despite the considerable commitment required, I believe that participating in the community as a full member allowed me not only to collect valuable information about the fansubbers' workflow and organisation, which would otherwise have

DOI: 10.1057/9781137470379.0004

been impossible for me to obtain, but also to develop a wider perspective concerning the phenomenon.

The present research study builds on prior research concerning amateur translation conducted by Bogucki, and found in Díaz-Cintas and Anderman's *Audiovisual Translation: Language Transfer on Screen* (2009). In his paper, *Amateur Subtitling on the Internet*, the author affirms that the rise of crowdsourcing was due to the widespread use of internet technologies, thanks to the advent of Web 2.0, the so-called "web revolution" giving rise to a new audiovisual translation mode, that of amateur subtitling. After a brief overview of the phenomenon, Bogucki made it clear that the problem with fansubbing,

> lies not so much in squeezing the gist of what the original characters say into 30 or so characters per line [...]; the problem, it seems, lies mostly in the quality of the source material and the competence and expertise of the translators.

(2009:50)

In the concluding remarks of his paper, the author ultimately deems the work of fansubbers to be unfeasible, since the lack of access to original scripts makes their work highly unpredictable, while their linguistic incompetence severely undermines its credibility. However, he also argues that if amateur subtitling were to reach near-professional standards, the resulting fansubs could be subjected to translation quality assessment and thus contrasted with professional subtitling. Since the quality of Italian fansubbing translations has greatly improved with time, being produced under conditions almost comparable with those found in a professional environment, as well as fulfilling the requirements proposed by Bogucki, continued research into the field was felt to be appropriate.

The phenomenon under analysis, in which emphasis is placed on the amateur translation of American TV series, has mainly emerged as a response to the demands of fans, primarily as a means of avoiding the long waits between seasons due to bureaucratic processes, as well as an alternative to dubbing, which is nowadays perceived as an outmoded, unreliable and ultimately unsuitable mode of audiovisual transfer. The key factor in the phenomenon under analysis is the growth of the Internet, with its almost infinite storage capacity, enabling anyone to watch, download and upload a wide selection of content. This is the reason why, during the past decade, with the widespread use of the Internet, along with the advent of Web 2.0, younger generations of Italians have come into closer contact with American

DOI: 10.1057/9781137470379.0004

culture. Being exposed to US TV programmes in their original version on a daily basis, they began to perceive that the Italian dubbed versions, addressed to a stereotyped, homogeneous and monolithic audience, had undergone a process of "nationalisation" (Danan 1999), which was no longer acceptable.

According to Cantor and Cantor (1986), "programmers care primarily that their product appeals to large numbers of viewers [...] and care little about the meanings, significance, or ritual that television fulfils as a cultural product to a core audience of dedicated fans". Italian fans have, in some way, felt betrayed and grossly underestimated by the policies of these dubbing companies. They have felt compelled to take the lead in the current Internet revolution by gradually developing into organised communities capable of creating their own alternative modes of translation for themselves. Guided by the subculture surrounding fandom, fans have abandoned mainstream broadcasting channels in order to experiment with unconventional pathways built by grassroots networks of fans, the most popular of all being ItaSA (www.italiansub.net), immediately followed by Subsfactory (www.subsfactory.it).

In this book, the phenomenon of Italian fansubbing is examined from its origins until now (see Chapters 3, 4, 5, 6) in order to understand the profound transformations experienced by Italian audiovisual translation to date. The focus of this research project primarily involves the context within which the fansubbing revolution began, followed by a review of the fandom and "co-creational labour" (Banks 2009) seen from the perspective of Media Studies. According to Banks, formerly passive TV consumers have ended up becoming the primary actors in a major revolution, a collective subculture able to resist the hegemony of more powerful institutions (Jenkins 1992).

Having contextualised the phenomenon from the angle of Media Studies, in the third chapter the driving forces at the roots of this practice are examined, namely the creation of the first online communities, their hierarchical structure and the roles adopted by fansubbers along with the protocols and the technicalities employed in order to edit, produce and release the fansubbed versions of the shows. In Chapter 4, the comparisons between subtitling and fansubbing norms are investigated, as well as the ideological aspects of this phenomenon.

In the light of the theories propounded by Lewis (1985), Nornes (1999) and Venuti (2008), relevance is given to the approach employed by fansubbers, an approach which relates to "foreignisation" and "target-orientedness" as opposed to "domestication", which is the

DOI: 10.1057/9781137470379.0004

guiding principle of mainstream subtitling. The last section in the chapter focuses on subtitling based on brand new guidelines deriving from a hybrid approach to both fansubbing and mainstream practices. A "hybrid proposal", resulting from the merging of both the professional and the fansubbing worlds, should aim to take into account the needs of the viewer, while striking a balance between professional standards and common sense. A set of norms with these features might, indeed, be welcomed by a wider audience of Italian viewers who might choose to opt for subtitling instead of dubbing.

In Chapter 5, a number of case studies have been described in order to examine the main features of amateur subtitling, providing evidence for the evolution of the communities under analysis in terms of quality and workflow organisation. The first case study focuses on *Lost*, a sci-fi TV programme with a complex, nonlinear storyline developed with an extensive use of the "flash-sideways" technique and a multiple narrative perspective device known as "polyphonic narrative" (Cate 2009). The case study in question is a comparative analysis of episode 1 of the second season and episode 1 of the final season of *Lost* aiming to identify the key features of fansubbing and trace the evolution of amateurs' methodologies over time.

The second case study addresses the topics of censorship and humour, as well as the *défaillances* of both fansubbers and professionals. It is an analysis of the pilot episode of *Californication* (first aired on *Showtime* in 2007), a US TV series treating the life of a novelist *à la* Bukowski dealing with a writer's block as well as battling with his addictions: sex, drugs and alcohol, a set of hot topics expressed in a rather explicit language. Through a set of examples based on the failings of professional audiovisual translators, there has also been an attempt to emphasise and discuss the reasons for the deepening crisis in the subtitling market, as well as the current transformation in the role of the subtitler. Awkward though the failings of professionals may be, they clearly indicate that the sphere of professional translation is undergoing a critical phase, or as Gee and Hayes put it, "the crisis of the experts" (2011:44). Thus, the conclusions derived from this study transcend a merely qualitative linguistic analysis to encompass a wide range of sociological aspects relating to the status of professional translators and the professional opportunities facing translators in the future.

The book concludes with a consideration of fansubbing and the new avenue of research connected with this study. By way of conclusion, it

DOI: 10.1057/9781137470379.0004

is argued that Italian fansubbing has led to a redefinition of subtitling standards by both professionals and academics. Indeed, the reshaping of subtitling norms – a hybridisation of approaches, merging professional and fansubbing conventions – might be advisable and is likely to happen in the future, and it might also represent an interesting trend concerning research into Translation Studies, and Audiovisual Translation Studies in particular, which is likely to be forthcoming in the future.

0.1 Context and methodology

The process of devising a methodological framework for the research is dealt with in the introductory chapter of this book. The multidisciplinary approach adopted here necessitated an investigation of different theoretical and methodological approaches, since the study includes both empirical and speculative components, namely the theoretical investigation concerning norms in mainstream subtitling and fansubbing, and the linguistic observation carried out in the comparative case studies described in Chapters 5, 6 and 7. Therefore, the speculative and practical nature of the project needed to be contextualised and placed within definitive areas of research within Translation Studies as a discipline.

The motivating force behind this research study was if, and to what extent, fansubbing has influenced audiovisual translation practices in Italy. It also includes the dominant inquiry posed in this project, the question which is recurrent in every section of the book, which we have attempted to answer from a cultural, sociological and professional perspective. The first step involved in the process was the selection of the audiovisual material to be investigated, material which included a large archive of fansubs (belonging to ItaSA and Subsfactory), videos and DVDs with multilingual features needing to be scanned in search of salient features peculiar to fansubbing, as well as being useful in order to make parallels with subtitling. Needless to say, the data collection stage proved to be relatively long and laborious, since it involved viewing three versions (ItaSA's, Subsfactory's and DVD version) of the same audiovisual product several times.

In order to exemplify the empirical methodology adopted during this phase, a screenshot has been included, showing the organisation of a number of videos and text files as they appeared on the computer screen

DOI: 10.1057/9781137470379.0004

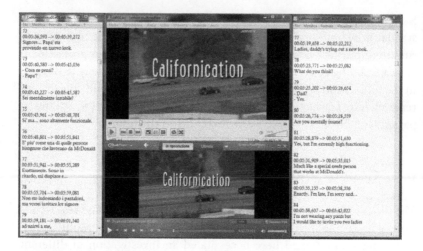

FIGURE 0.1   *Comparative analysis of Californication*

during an examination of an episode of one of the TV series under analysis (see Figure 0.1).

For the purpose of this research, the approach devised was of a qualitative rather than a quantitative nature, even though a quantitative approach was adopted initially by emailing a set of questionnaires to both ItaSA and Subsfactory in order to acquire information about fansubbing communities. Unfortunately, this technique was not favourably welcomed by the fansubbers themselves, so we were forced to resort to different methods of investigation more in tune with the research context. It was thus decided to adopt a qualitative paradigm consisting of interviews and direct observations, owing to the fact that by developing a more informal approach it was possible to come into closer contact with these underground subtitling factories. Once established, the relationship with the amateur translators went on to become a quasi-professional commitment, since it was concluded that, in order to understand the phenomenon fully, it was necessary to join the two communities in the role of fansubber.

0.2   Reflections on theory

In this section, the various theoretical approaches employed in the research are examined.

DOI: 10.1057/9781137470379.0004

In previous research focusing on audiovisual translation (cf. Luyken et al, 1991; Ivarsson, 1992; Gottlieb, 1998; Ivarsson and Carroll, 1998; Kovacic, 1991; De Linde and Kay 1999; Díaz Cintas, 2001 and 2003; Chaume, 2004; Díaz Cintas and Remael, 2007; Georgakopoulou, 2003), an approach in which the study was carried out using a combination of subtitle translations and back translations was used in order to find out whether the core meaning, style and register of the original had been conveyed into the target text. Drawing on this research pattern, the design of the empirical study proposed is a comparative analysis of different translations of the same source text, focusing on particular aspects relating to subtitling strategies, such as omission, deletion and adaptation, but also to other characteristics such as mistranslation, style and register, undertranslation, faithfulness to the source text and accuracy.

Toury's Descriptive Translation Studies (1995) was selected as what we considered the most suitable approach for a comparative methodology of analysis, as it sheds light on the norms at work in the translation process in general. Holmes' map of translation studies (1972; 1988) formed the basis of Toury's Descriptive Translation Studies (DTS), considered as one of the two main fields in Translation Studies, the first centred on the empirical description of translation phenomena, and the other focused on the theorisation of principles.

As suggested by Holmes, the branch of DTS, in turn, is further divided into three sub areas: "product-oriented", "function-oriented" and "process-oriented". As far as this research is concerned, "product-oriented" DTS has been used during the examination of existing translations, an examination which involved a source text (ST) – target text (TT) comparative analysis of several versions of the same text. However, as stated by Toury, the three branches in question are strictly interdependent and a thorough investigation requires a wider perspective embracing the three aspects of DTS noted above.

Seen in this light, the "function-oriented" type of DTS, served to analyse the research context from a social-cultural point of view, and the "process-oriented" DTS, came into play during the attempt made to understand the reasons behind the translational choices made by subtitlers. The results of the comparative analysis based on DTS were eventually fed into the theoretical aspects of the research project, namely those relating to the study of norms and conventions in subtiling and fansubbing. Therefore, drawing on the initial empirical analysis, a

DOI: 10.1057/9781137470379.0004

particular emphasis has been placed on the specific norms at work in subtitling and fansubbing, in an attempt to describe the possible evolution of mainstream conventions as a result of the empirical observation of translational behaviour (Pedersen 2011).

The issue of translation norms in general, has attracted the interest of researchers over the past few years (cf. Carroll 2004; Chesterman 1993, 1997, 1998; Georgakopoulou 2003; Hermans 1991, 1996, 1999; Ivarsson 1992; Ivarsson and Carroll 1998; Karamitroglou 1998, 2000; Nord 1991, 1997; Pedersen 2011; Pym, Shlesinger & Simeoni 2008; Toury 1980). Toury (1980; 1995) regarded translation as an activity governed by specific norms which he categorised as "initial norms", "preliminary norms" and "operational norms". "Initial norms" involve the selection on the part of the translators either of norms related to the source language or the target language with a closer adherence to source language norms leading to translation "adequacy" as far as the source text is concerned, whereas "acceptability" in the target language culture is reached when translators adhere to the norms of the receiving culture. "Preliminary norms", on the other hand, focus on the choice of the source text (text typology and language, for example) and "operational norms" govern the process of translation. In turn, they are subdivided into "matricial" (centred on the omission and deletion of the target text) and "textual-linguistic" norms (focused on language and style). Conversely, Hermans (1999) proposed an alternative to Toury's notions of "adequacy" and "acceptability", using the expressions: "source-oriented" and "target-oriented" respectively. Hermans' approach to norms, together with Chesterman's reformulation of Toury's norms will form the methodological framework of this study. However, since there is no mutual consensus of opinion as far as the term "norm" is concerned, in the present study Chesterman's concept of "expectancy norms" (1997) has been used, a fact which is apparently central to the approach adopted here, since they emanate precisely from what viewers expect and above all demand: "expectancy norms are established by the expectations of readers of a translation (of a given type) concerning what a translation (of this type) should be like" (1997:64).

According to Chesterman's dichotomy, "expectancy norms" indicate the audience's expectations concerning subtitled products, while "professional norms" refer to the rules universally accepted by translators (cf. Sokoli 2011). Chesterman holds the belief that readers are able to perceive what is either appropriate or inappropriate in the translation of a certain text typology, thus approving of the fulfilment of expectations related to

DOI: 10.1057/9781137470379.0004

translation. In fact, as the author of this work has posited, at times there may be no shared consensus of opinion regarding the norms imposed by the established authority.

The research departs at precisely this point, since we have speculated regarding the manner in which fansubbing emerged in resistance to both dubbing adaptation and mainstream subtitling conventions. The niche audience of TV show fans has, in fact, permitted us to perceive mainstream conventions as outmoded, inadequate and above all excessively "target-oriented". In other words, "target-oriented" translation norms are blamed for altering relevant aspects of signification, idioms, register and style, and also for impoverishing the sense of otherness inherent in the foreign dialogue in the name of fluency, readability and the questionable notion of transparency. Against this background, it has been decided to employ a "source-oriented" approach as constituting the core theoretical framework for this study, a method inspired by the work of Lewis (1985), Nornes (1999) and Venuti (2008). The dichotomy between "domestication" and "foreignisation" is further explained in Venuti's *The Translator's Invisibility* (2008), in which the author, following Schleiermacher's theories, envisages an approach which gives prominence to the cultural and linguistic difference of the source text, noting that the translator should "leave the author in peace and move the reader towards him" (ibid.:19). In contrast with the dominant domesticating approaches to translation, he calls for a theory of the "visible translator", a theory that is able to counteract and resist "dominant target-language cultural values in order to convey the foreignness of the original text" (ibid.:23).

Lewis' concept of "abusive fidelity" further amplifies Venuti's ideological theories on translation:

> Abusive fidelity directs the translator's attention away from the conceptual signified to the play of signifiers on which it depends, to phonological, syntactical, and discursive structures, resulting in a translation that values experimentation, tampers with usage, seeks to match the polyvalencies or plurivocities or expressive stresses of the original by producing its own.
>
> (ibid.:24)

The experimental strategies proposed by Lewis and involving various aspects of translation, register, dialect, style and lexicon, for instance, consistently adhere to the fansubbers' philosophy of translation. In their adherence to the linguistic and cultural features of the source text, fansubbers, the "abusive translators", represent the genuine application

DOI: 10.1057/9781137470379.0004

of the "foreignising" theories described above. Fansubbers are not simply "literal" in their approach to translation, yet in the light of the above, they are almost revolutionary, as confirmed by Nornes and his "abusive subtiling theory" (2004).

According to Nornes (1999), the "corrupt practices" of mainstream subtitling aim to hide the alterity of the original audiovisual product by conforming to the values, language and culture of the target audience. The umbrella term "corruption" embraces a variety of translational behaviours defined by Danan (1991) as "nationalisation", for example, the frequent practice prevalent in Italian audiovisual translation of appropriating the source text by converting foreign popular names into their target text equivalents, even though the audience would be able to understand them perfectly. These corrupt practices entail the reduced freedom of translators on different levels. Freelance subtitlers, in fact, are often requested to work on "templates" – made for a potential "world audience" rather than a specific audience (cf. Georgakopolou 2003) – where time codes have already been established, so that they simply replace the source by the target language. Needless to say, this modus operandi, meant to cut the costs (e.g., software dongles), is also a way of retaining obsolete norms, set during the age of the Hollywood studio system (cf. Nornes 1999; Díaz-Cintas 2012). In fact, the inability to perform the cueing process results in an added curtailment of the translator's already limited freedom. Díaz-Cintas argued that:

> When the timing has been done by a professional other than the translator, the latter's freedom can be severely restricted. [...] if translators could do their own spotting, they could be more flexible and make a more rational use of the spaces needed for any given subtitle.
>
> (2012:2–3)

Similarly, Georgakopoulou highlighted the fact that "thanks to the development of dedicated subtitling software, subtitlers could [...] spot the film themselves and then write their translations so as to fit the time slots they had spotted" (2006:30). Since they work outside the professional translation industry, fansubbers, on the other hand, are able to fulfil the role of both "synchers" and translators, and as a result, are responsible for and in greater control of the whole subtitling process.

Therefore, whether we define our methodological framework as "source-oriented", "foreignised, or "abusive", the central idea is to move away from a fluent, domesticated, transparent translation to an "overt" kind of translation (House 1977), in order to preserve the cultural and linguistic flavour of the original. Thus, not only is the methodological approach used here openly "source-oriented", but also "viewer-centred", since the end-viewers, with their growing demands for a revolution in the niche area of subtitling TV shows, are central to the reshaping of subtitling norms. According to Hermans, "norms change because they need to be constantly readjusted so as to meet changing appropriateness conditions" (1999:84).

In conclusion, a methodological overview of the multi-layered approach employed in the investigation of the theory and practices adopted by the Italian fansubbing communities is provided in this section. Much has been drawn from the systems theories related to translation, in particular from Toury's Descriptive Translation Studies (1995) and Chesterman's subsequent studies regarding norms (1997), with special reference to the notion of "expectancy norms".

In addition, the different approaches belonging to the ideologies under examination within the field of Translation Studies, including the dichotomy between "domestication" and "foreignisation" examined by Schleiermacher (1813), Lewis' "abusive fidelity" (1985), Venuti's concept of the translator's "visibility" (2008) and Nornes's "abusive subtitling" (1999) all concurred to clarify the orientation adopted by the fansubbing communities for their translations. Not only were they paramount in helping to categorise and analyse the phenomenon in depth, but also in determining a hybrid proposal – a set of future guidelines for subtitlers – derived from mainstream subtitling and fansubbing conventions (described in Chapter 4), considered as the main contribution of this study to academic research in the field of audiovisual translation and fan translation in particular.

Note

1   "Subber in prova", or would-be fansubber, the equivalent of "junior translator" for *ItaSA*.

DOI: 10.1057/9781137470379.0004

1
Web 2.0: A Marketing Ideology?

Abstract: *The concept behind Web 2.0 represents the core topic for this section, a concept that focuses specifically on the groundbreaking phenomena of crowdsourcing and fansubbing. The democratisation of media production brought about by the technical and commercial revolution of Web 2.0 is thoroughly analysed in connection with digital labour (Google and Facebook, for example). A further insight into the issue of copyright infringement is offered in the second section of this chapter. The book derives from the Berne Convention for the Protection of Literary and Artistic Works to the EULA (End User License Agreement), the complex mechanism employed for strengthening copyright protection against piracy, shedding light on a grey area within a highly controversial system intended to fight crime, but, ultimately, resulting in a breach of copyright.*

Massidda, Serenella. *Audiovisual Translation in the Digital Age: The Italian Fansubbing Phenomenon.* Basingstoke: Palgrave Macmillan, 2015. DOI: 10.1057/9781137470379.0005.

DOI: 10.1057/9781137470379.0005

1.1 Digital labour in the age of prosumers

We get all the culture; they get all the revenue.

McKenzie Wark (2012)

A variety of digital tools for a new "participatory culture" (Jenkins 2008) has emerged over the past few years: indeed, neologisms such as "fansubbing" and "crowdsourcing" have now entered the popular lexicon. In an attempt to discuss the logic behind these two apparently interchangeable phenomena, we will introduce the specific context in which they originated.

Following Fernández Costales, "on the basis of the free and – almost – universal access to information, the process known as collaborative translation has gained momentum in the last decade in parallel to the professional practice of translation" (2012:116). The link between these neologisms is the democratisation of media production brought about by the technical and commercial revolution referred to as "Web 2.0", a concept introduced for the first time by DiNucci and then "reprised", intertwined with the topic of fan translation, by many scholars (cf. Baym 2009; Bassett 2013; Bogucki, 2009; Bold 2012; Boyd 2014; Chronin 2013. Dwyer 2012; Fernández Costales 2011; Kayahara 2005; Keen 2007; Lovink & Rash 2013; O'Hagan 2009, 2011a, 2011b; Napoli 2010; Pérez-González & Susam-Saraeva 2012; Pérez-González 2013; Sevignani & Fuchs 2013; Sützl, Stalder, Maier & Hug 2012).

In her 1999 article, entitled "Fragmented Future", DiNucci explained that:

> The Web we know now [...] is only an embryo of the Web to come. The first glimmerings of Web 2.0 are beginning to appear, and we are just starting to see how that embryo might develop. The Web will be understood not as screenfuls of text and graphics but as a transport mechanism, the ether through which interactivity happens.
>
> (DiNucci 1999:1)

According to De Kosnik,

> personalization is one of the key promises of postindustrial capitalism, since [...] the niche marketing, narrowcasting, and two-way communication facilitated by the web [2.0] all promise to give consumers exactly what each of them wants.
>
> (2013:1)

DOI: 10.1057/9781137470379.0005

The first Web 2.0 conference, organised by John Battelle and Tim O'Reilly, was held in 2004. In their opening remarks, they confirmed that "the unique aspect of this migration [...] is that customers are building your business for you", highlighting the fact that Web 2.0 is fundamentally a marketing ideology. In fact, "ubiquitous computing" (Cronin 2010) in the digital era has given way to "web-as-participation-platforms" (Decrem 2006) exemplified by user-generated content websites (YouTube, for example), and social-networking sites such as Facebook, wikis and blogs, where traditionally passive users have been encouraged to interact, becoming active "prosumers" (Toffler 1980). Originally coined to define the ambiguous role played by consumers intervening in the production process, this portmanteau of "producer" and "consumer" is also applicable to the "proactive" users who have become the real protagonists of the digital revolution, participating in the transformation of goods and services offered by digital multimedia systems.

The "co-creative labour" of fans (Banks and Deuze 2009) generated by the Internet revolution has led to some predictable outcomes aptly summarised by Scholtz in *Digital Labour – The Internet as Playground and Factory* (2013), a collection of articles discussing "digital labour", a dual concept perpetually swinging between "work" and "play". This ambiguity is a "trademark" of Google: its unconventional workspace, where the best engineers collaborate in an informal atmosphere with plenty of free food and games rooms, is a clear attempt to demonstrate that work and play can exist side by side. This confusing notion goes far beyond this fact, embracing the notion not only of regular but also "unpaid employees", even if Google proudly claims to put users first.

As a matter of fact, Fuchs explains that:

> Google [...] exploits and monitors users by selling their data to advertising clients. Half [...] of all people using the Internet access Google, and that is roughly 1.05 billion people [...]. Google would not exist without these users because its profits are based on ads targeted to searches, which means that the search process is value-generating. Google's more than 1 billion users are [...] largely lacking financial compensation. They perform unpaid, value-generating labour.
>
> (2013:2)

On the occasion of "Multimedia Translation in the Digital Age",[1] an event recently held by The Centre for Translation Studies at University College London and chaired by Jorge Díaz-Cintas, O'Hagan covered the debated issue of "fan labour", focusing on the difference between translation crowdsourcing and fan translation. She made it clear that translation in the digital age is becoming "for anyone by everyone", and that its quality is "fit-for-purpose" depending on that particular purpose or "skopos" (Vermeer 1989).

The term "fansubbing", which literally defines the activity of "fans producing fansubs for other fans" (Díaz-Cintas and Sánchez 2006) is one of the most widespread forms of amateur translation on the Internet. The tradition of fansubbing started in the 1980s when Japanese "anime" were banned in the United States due to their inappropriate content. Yet, as confirmed by Dwyer, "current research on fansubbing is broadened by examining this phenomenon beyond the strictures of anime subculture alone [...] and exploring the gaps in mainstream subtitling that fansubbing both exposes and fills" (2012:1).

Nowadays, "Internet crowds" (O'Hagan 2014) busy themselves translating US TV shows "thanks to the possibility of exchanging information on a free basis and in real time" (Fernández Costales 2011:1). Individual and altruistic motives are at the roots of fan translation: "DIY communities" (Paulos 2013) translate in order to reduce the delays or to make up for the total lack of official translations by releasing the fansubs within a couple of days after the airdate; as a reaction to the inaccuracy and excessive manipulation of official translations (Italian dubbing, for example), and also as a form of recreation, or "playbour" (a mixture of "play" and "labour") as defined by Scholtz (2013).

On the other hand, the concept of "crowdsourcing" is closely related to the exploitation of the "wisdom of crowds" (Surowiecki 2005). In *The Wisdom of Crowds*, using a fine example, Surowiecki demonstrated how the intelligence of many could be worth millions of pounds. In the popular TV game show *Who wants to be a Millionaire?*, the contestants can appeal to an expert by phone or poll the studio audience. It turns out that "those random crowds of people with nothing better to do on a weekday afternoon than sit in a TV studio, picked the right answer 91 percent of the time" (ibid.:4).

The same logical reasoning lies behind the foundation of Web 2.0, and it is extremely effective: this is exactly what Mark Zuckerberg had in mind when he decided to launch the Translation App on Facebook. On the home page of the Translation Application Guide we find the following disclaimer:

DOI: 10.1057/9781137470379.0005

> Volunteer translators make it possible for us to make Facebook available in many languages around the world. First of all, thank you for your interest and contributions. You are helping to make Facebook accessible to a lot of people! The purpose of this guide is to show you how to use the translation app and introduce its main features. We hope you will enjoy using the app and this Translation App Guide.[2]

The above message shows the strategic choice of expressions in the disclaimer notices issued by the company: "volunteer translators", "make Facebook available", "interest and contribution", "help make Facebook accessible", "hope you will enjoy the app". Evidently, Facebook Inc. seems to confuse "labour" and "play", "enjoinment" and "work", "translation app" and "translation job".

With their elegant approach, Facebook has offered its users the unique chance to have fun translating their social networking site into more than 70 languages. In turn, other users have evaluated Facebook's top translations by voting with a simple click in order for top translators to unlock their rewards, just like a game. Web 2.0 user-tailorable technology, allowing good workflow management, has made the project a major success.

"Crowdsourcing" is characterised by users' "participation in a voluntary, self-selected activity launched as a form of problem-solving" (O'Hagan 2014), in the style of *Who wants to be a Millionaire?*. The call for help does not come from an unknown contestant participating in a game show, however, but from powerful multinational corporations. In fact, another way of looking at the phenomena of "fansubbing" and "crowdsourcing" is through copyright infringement. While fansubbing is a grassroots activity based on the illegal adaptation of an artistic work, crowdsourcing represents an act of a company launching an open call in order to outsource digital labour to a network of "undefined people" (Howe 2009), and in the best case scenario, for free. In other words, while crowdsourcing is a legal, unethical activity, fansubbing is an illegal, ethical activity (O'Hagan 2014). While in crowdsourcing, copyright holders exploit the digital labour of specialised users to make a profit, the practice of fansubbing is based on the production and distribution of unauthorised translations of copyrighted audiovisual materials without financial compensation.

Fan translation is therefore ethical because it is intended as an unselfish activity, a form of social disobedience, and a reaction to professional

DOI: 10.1057/9781137470379.0005

translations that do not meet fans' needs (O'Hagan 2014). According to Rembert-Lang,

> selling fansub translations is frowned upon in the fansubbing community and is considered bootlegging. There are, however, live streaming websites and torrent sites that have fansub translations of television programs and movies and accept donations as gifts for running their websites.
>
> (2010:4)

Yet, from whatever angle we look at it, the key concept is that fans' expertise is not worth paying for. In her blog, spreadablemedia.org, De Kosnik writes:

> [...] as long as they do not sell their works, they will be safe from legal persecution. Conventional wisdom holds that companies and individuals that own the copyrights to mass-media texts will not sue fan producers, as long as the fans do not make money from their works.
>
> (2013:1)

This is the deal, and fans accept it as long as they can continue their underground activity undisturbed. However, it is a pretty good deal for copyright holders too since co-creative labour "[...] can rampup the buzz and reputation of a product [...]", as a new form of advertising (De Kosnik 2012:109). The intense work undertaken by fansubbers attracts, generates and retains the interest of fans of a specific TV show and, in addition, it also represents a means of deciding the success of a TV product: if the first season of a show turns out to be popular among fans, then its copyright will be acquired by both public and private TV channels. As De Kosnik argues further,

> the customization work that fans perform on media productions also serves to educate the [...] industries about consumer preferences, thereby serving as a free source of potentially valuable audience research for media companies.
>
> (2013:1)

In addition, fans have also proved to have the right to question professional translations of their favourite programmes. This aspect was thoroughly investigated by Innocenti and Maestri in their paper, "Il lavoro dei fan. Il fansubbing come alternativa al doppiaggio ufficiale in *The Big Bang Theory*" (2010) in which the authors explore this popular TV show focusing on the phenomenon of fansubbing as an alternative to dubbing.

DOI: 10.1057/9781137470379.0005

The Big Bang Theory (first aired on CBS in 2007) is a sit-com starring four characters similar to the very fans under analysis: they are nerds just like fansubbers. Once Mediaset had acquired the copyright for the show, the programme was dubbed by Post in Europe (PIE) in Rome and broadcast on the pay-TV channel Steel in 2008. Having followed the first season with fansubs, when fans watched the Italian dubbing version, to their amazement, they realised that the language had been levelled down to such an extent that it was almost unrecognisable and did not appeal at all to the target audience who criticised the work of the dubbing company harshly. Owing to the "italianisation" of the dubbed version, the whole nerdy-related content had been dumbed down, making the product unbearably dull.

In order to describe the mistakes found in the dubbed versions under analysis, an example is offered in Table 1.1.

The adaptation carried out in the dialogue, and displayed in Table 1.1, is rather interesting when Sheldon closes the exchange. While we may agree with the fact that "Fuddruckers", a fast food chain almost unknown in Italy, is a US cultural-bound reference that needs to be adapted to suit the target language in question, the most obvious choice to translate it as "McDonalds" or "Burger King" was not employed and for no apparent

TABLE 1.1   *The Big Bang Theory – season 1, episode 1*

Original Dialogue

Sheldon: Leonard, I don't think I can do this.
Leonard: *What, are you kidding? You're a semi-pro.*
Sheldon: No, we are committing genetic fraud. There's no guarantee that our sperm's going to generate high-IQ offspring, think about that. I have a sister with the same basic DNA mix that hosts at Fuddruckers.

Dubbed Version

Sheldon: Leonard, io non posso farlo.
Leonard: Scherzi? Sei un **semi-donatore**, ormai.
Sheldon: No, questa è frode genetica vera e propria. Che garanzia c'è che dal nostro seme venga generata prole superintelligente? **Mia sorella disse le prime parole a sei anni e fece la stessa classe 5 volte**.

Back Translation

Sheldon: Leonard, I cannot do this.
Leonard: Leonard: Are you kidding? You are a semi-donator.
Sheldon: No, this is genetic fraud, true and real. What is the guarantee that from our sperm we generate super intelligent offspring? My sister pronounced her first words at six and repeated the same grade five times.

DOI: 10.1057/9781137470379.0005

reason. In fact, owing to the fact that Sheldon has a twin sister (they, thus, share the same DNA), the dialogue could have been understood without unnecessary transformation. In addition, the likelihood that a schoolgirl will repeat the same grade five times in Italy is quite remote, a fact which adds to the oddity of the Italian adaptation and the resulting absence of the intended comic effect. Hence, a bitter controversy carried out by fans of *The Big Bang Theory* sparked several online blogs in Italy leading to dramatic changes to the dubbed production. From episode nine of the first season, the dubbing director, Silvia Pepitoni, was replaced by Leslie La Penna and the whole team of adaptors was entirely replaced. As a result, the new team carried out a better adaptation, characterised by a more faithful and coherent dialogue. The effective resistance of the Italian active audience made it clear that the patronising authority of the dubbing technique has been losing its grip and in the light of the analysis carried out by Innocenti and Maestri, and according to Vellar (2011:8), "subbers are now recognised as experts by fan cultures and by mass media" (see Chapter 3 on the organised fan industry for an in-depth analysis).

1.2   What is copyright?

The issue of legality was alluded to briefly in the opening of this chapter: in the previous section, in fact, we have hinted at the supposed illegal, ethical activity carried out by fansubbers. In order to distance themselves from such allegations, fansubbers have chosen to produce the so called "soft subs" rather than working with "hard subs" (see Chapter 3, section 1), an excellent choice considering the law that governs copyright. Soft subs, in fact, unlike hard subs, which are merged with the video clip, are .srt files which are separate from the video and that can be loaded by users onto specific video players. Hence, the choice of soft subs for fansubbing purposes is largely due to the threat represented by copyright infringement. In the disclaimer section of its forum, ItaSA makes it clear that:

> All downloadable content in this website is absolutely free. The translations available, in accordance with the current regulations, are a free interpretation by our translators and therefore protected by law. The content available does not include any copyrighted video or link to proprietary materials.[3]

DOI: 10.1057/9781137470379.0005

And on its homepage, Subsfactory offers the following assurance:

> The website does not infringe copyright and it is 100% legal, as the transla-
> tions provided are a free interpretation by our translators to whom we are
> deeply grateful! Merging the .srt files we provide with the copyrighted video
> is contrary to the spirit in which they have been produced, besides being
> against the law.[4]

In conclusion, what Italian fansubbers do is to release a translation
conceived as a personal interpretation of a TV programme in order to
share it with fellow fans. As a result, the way fans retrieve the copyrighted
video associated with the fansubs is therefore irrelevant to them. Having
explained fansubbers' modus operandi as far as the issue of copyright
infringements is concerned, now we will consider the regulations in
force.

According to Rembert-Lang, "Laws governing international copyright
law include: The Berne Convention, the Uruguay Round Agreements Act
(URAA),[5] and the Universal Copyright Convention (UCC)[6]" (2010:6–7).
In the "Berne Convention for the Protection of Literary and Artistic
Works" we read that:

> Copyright is a legal term used to describe the rights that creators have over
> their literary and artistic works. Works covered by copyright range from
> books, music, paintings, sculpture and films, to computer programs, data-
> bases, advertisements, maps and technical drawings.[7]

As far as translation is concerned, two articles of the "Berne Convention
for the Protection of Literary and Artistic Works" are worth citing:
article 2 and 8. Article 8 of the Berne Convention, entitled "Right of
Translation", provides: "Artists of literary and artistic work shall enjoy
the exclusive right of making and of authorizing the translation of their
works throughout the term of protection of their rights in original
works". However, in article 2, entitled "Protected Works" (section 3 on
"Derivative works"), we find that "translations, adaptations, arrange-
ments of music and other alterations of a literary or artistic work shall
be protected as original works without prejudice to the copyright in the
original work". Evidently, there is a grey area in between the two state-
ments cited, particularly as far as fan translation in general and fansubbing in particular are concerned.

Conversely, in the game localisation industry, this issue has already
been addressed. In fact, the profitable approach employed by the software

DOI: 10.1057/9781137470379.0005

industry has a specific name: EULA (End User License Agreement). According to Mangiron and O'Hagan, another neologism plays a fundamental role in the equation, "modding", which "[...] represents the most illustrative example of deep user engagement" (2013:296). "Modding" is the act of illegally modifying software programs in order to customise the original content of videogames. Additionally, in the gaming community, the altered content is subsequently illegally shared online. In reaction to modding activities, the gaming industry has secured a digital contract between the copyright owner and the user in order to define how the software can be used. The agreement is a click-wrap license frequently presented on-screen during installation: the user must click on "accept" in order to complete the purchase process.

To some extent, EULA may be considered an attempt to widen the licensor's control over software copyright, which has some grey areas and limitations as well, particularly as far as sections 107–122 of the United States Copyright Act are concerned. In order to exemplify the purpose of EULA, in Apple's Licensed Application End User License Agreement, we read that "You agree not to modify, rent, lease, loan, sell, distribute, or create derivative works based on the Services, in any manner".[8] In conclusion, according to Mangiron and O'Hagan, "the EULA is [also] the game industry's way of plugging into [...] user's creativity without adversely impacting their own business" (ibid:307).

1.3   Piracy or promotion? The history of fansubbing

> *"Traditionally, it has been implicitly acknowledged by fansubbers, as well as by Japanese copyright holders, that the free distribution of fansubs can have a very positive impact in the promotion of a given anime series in other countries."*
>
> (Díaz Cintas and Muñoz Sánchez 2006:8)

As already noted in the first section of this chapter, the impact of fansubbing on the promotion of the vast majority of American TV shows in Italy is no secret. What was said in the past concerning other underground practices can easily be applied to this new phenomenon. According to Lessig (2004:27), "major media in the US, including films, recorded music, and cable TV, all depended heavily on piracy for their early success". Popular culture industries such as Japanese anime have greatly benefited from fansubbing, as is shown by the almost total absence of

DOI: 10.1057/9781137470379.0005

legal actions taken against it. In a recent interview, Superbiagi, one of Subsfactory's administrators, advises users against associating subtitles with copyrighted videos, with the assurance that:

> Our website does not have the numbers or the false pretences to undermine the market of audiovisual translation. If we are supposed to challenge professional subtitling, how come that SKY has not hired us yet?[9]

Yet, the fact that on Italian satellite channels the gap between seasons has been significantly reduced is due to the underground work of these passionate fans. Thus, even if they represent the proverbial drop in the ocean, to some extent what they do really matters. According to Casarini,

> some Italian networks (most notably, Sky Italia) have started to respond to these new needs, offering their viewers a subtitled versions of recently-aired episodes of US shows and promoting an unprecedented acceleration of the dubbing process.
>
> (2014:15)

These communities, averaging 1,000 daily active users, nearly 23,000 (Subsfactory) and 55,000 (ItaSA) fans on Facebook, and a record of 7,000 downloads in a few hours, inevitably play a decisive role in the success of the programmes they translate. Not only do subbers make up for the time lag characteristic of dubbing, but in doing so, they also control the success of future TV shows, owing to the quality and speed with which they work.

In order to analyse this sheer incongruity between piracy and promotion, we need to go back to the 1980s, when fansubbing made its first appearance with the translation of Japanese anime. Following Kearns, "the earliest known reported fansub in the United States is said to be the VHS version of Lupin III produced in the mid-80s" (2008:161). The history of fansubbing, in fact, can be traced back to the late 1980s (O'Hagan 2009) when Japanese anime, the French abbreviation for "animation" (Leonard 2004), were banned or in some cases heavily censored in the United States due to their inappropriate content, a fact that lead to the Japanese withdrawal from the American market in 1982. As a consequence, fans of the genre began to gather in "anime clubs" devoted to the translation and distribution of their favourite animations. Fans began to produce amateur subtitled copies so that they could share them with their fellow fans. "At the time, the Internet had not as many users as it has nowadays, and these pioneers used to distribute fansubbed anime on videotapes rather than in digital format" (Díaz Cintas and Muñoz Sánchez 2006:8).

Before the digital era, fansubbers employed the "SASE system"[10] to disseminate their fansubs, a system through which tapes were mailed out to fans free of charge. With the advent of high-speed Web access, along with new software programs capable of editing and ripping DVDs, the SASE system was abandoned in favour of digital fansubbing or "digisubbing". Digisubs made their first appearance in the late 1990s, and were distributed through three main channels: P2P,[11] IRC[12] and Usenet. The most widespread P2P file sharing networks at the time were Bitorrent and Emule. BitTorrent allowed users to retrieve files on the net via the fansubbing group tracker (a web page displaying the link to .torrent files in order to download the fansubs), while Emule, on the other hand, was much slower than BitTorrent, and supported the searching of files by name using the ed2k network (Scarpa 2005). At the time, the most common form of IM[13] used by fansubbers was the IRC, a real time chat ideal for group communication, forum discussion and data transfer, including file sharing. Usenet was a hybrid between emails and web forums, where users could post as well as share content on the web. Moreover, several websites were dedicated to the distribution of fansubs. Some of the most popular were Animefactory,[14] the first to produce digisubs in .avi and DivX format, and Anime-Fansubs[15] – created in 2000 and still active – and Elite-Fansubs,[16] popular for having heated arguments with the online communities mentioned above (ibid.:2005).

Nowadays, with the advent of Web 2.0 and the widespread use of fast broadband Internet connection, fan experts may rely on secret groups on Facebook where they can communicate undisturbed, and retrieve the copyrighted material needed by downloading torrent files using software programs such as Utorrent, Wuze and the like. In fact, following the failure of Kim Dotcom's Megaupload, the most popular file hosting and sharing service ever created, fans have stopped using the direct link system for their purposes.

Interestingly, the author of "The Impact of Copyright Law on Fansubbing" looked at the issue of piracy from a different angle, stating that it is in fact the copyright law that represents a threat to co-creational activities:

DOI: 10.1057/9781137470379.0005

The social benefits that result from fansubbing activities outweigh any of the potential damages that could emerge because of copyright infringement and should entitle the activity to some form of protection under copyright law.

(Rembert-Lang 2010:14)

The author posited the creation of a "notice of use" in order to protect both the authors and the fansubbers. By using this method, a "translation right" can be created to give amateur translators a form of copyright for their derivative work:

The notice of use would require all fansub groups to send to television networks, producers, or artists of a respective television program or movie, a notice of use that specifies the intent to translate the prospective program or movie. The notice of use must be sent in the original language of the country of origin of television program or movie. The purpose and goal of this method is to place individuals on notice, and allow an informal right of translation.

(Rembert-Lang 2010:14–15)

We are of the opinion that this proposal might to some extent be viable, although it might also constitute the source of unexpected future consequences. However, it could also be argued that other illegal activities might exploit the notice of use in order to disobey the canons of copyright law based on legal precedent, thus establishing a rule for future cases.

Notes

1 Video contribution available at www.europe.org.uk/2014/07/10/multimedia-translation-in-the-digital-age-21may/.
2 www.facebook.com.
3 My translation. In the original: "I contenuti offerti dal portale sono interamente gratuiti. [Il sito contiene] traduzioni che, a norma delle vigenti leggi, sono interpretazioni dei traduttori e pertanto tutelate dal diritto vigente. Il sito non contiene filmati o link a file audiovideo coperti da copyright." *Source:* www.italiansubs.net.
4 My translation. In the original: "Il sito non infrange nessun copyright ed è legale al 100%, considerato che le traduzioni sono interpretazioni dei traduttori. si ringraziano tutti i subber per il loro fantastico lavoro!!! Subsfactory.it fornisce sottotitoli che sono una libera interpretazione dei

DOI: 10.1057/9781137470379.0005

traduttori, unirli a video e' scorretto ed e' contrario allo spirito per cui sono stati creati, oltre che illecito!". *Source:* www.subsfactory.it.

5   The Uruguay Round Agreements Act, Pub. L. No. 103–465, 108 Stat. 4809 (1994).

6   Universal Copyright Convention, revised, Paris, 24 July, 1971.

7   Full text available at www.wipo.int/treaties/en/text.jsp?file_id=283698.

8   www.apple.com/legal/internet-services/itunes/appstore/dev/stdeula/.

9   My translation. In the original: "Un sito come il nostro non ha i numeri né le pretese né la presunzione di poter influenzare il mercato dei traduttori. Se le nostre produzioni amatoriali togliessero effettivamente lavoro ai traduttori professionisti, perché allora *Sky* o chi per loro non ci ha assunti tutti?".

10   Self-Addressed Stamped Envelope.

11   Peer-to-peer, networking able to share workloads among peers.

12   Internet Relay Chat, a real-time text messaging and chat.

13   Instant Messaging, a form of real-time chatting communication.

14   www.animefactory.org.

15   www.anime-fansubs.net.

16   www.mayday-anime.com/forums.

DOI: 10.1057/9781137470379.0005

2

The State of the Art of Italian AVT: Dubbing Vis-à-Vis Subtitling

Abstract: *The main AVT modes adopted in Italy are examined in this section, highlighting the state of the art of these modes of transfer currently being challenged by the radical transformation experienced by the increasingly globalised film industry. After an introduction to the perennial dichotomy between dubbing and subtitling, the well-known classification between northern and southern European countries is analysed. While, in the first section, the tradition of dubbing in Italy is illustrated from the advent of the first silent "talkie" in the late 1920s until the present day, in the last section contemporary Italian subtitling industry is described, with a particular emphasis on the impact of changed market conditions, as well as the current professional identity crisis.*

Massidda, Serenella. *Audiovisual Translation in the Digital Age: The Italian Fansubbing Phenomenon.* Basingstoke: Palgrave Macmillan, 2015. DOI: 10.1057/9781137470379.0006.

DOI: 10.1057/9781137470379.0006

In this chapter, the main audiovisual translation modes adopted in Italy are examined, in an attempt to place them within their historical and cultural perspectives, while highlighting the state of the art of these modes of transfer which are currently being challenged by the radical transformation being experienced by the increasingly globalised film industry. After a brief introduction to the perennial dichotomy between dubbing and subtitling, the well-known classification between northern and southern European countries is analysed.

While, in the first section, the tradition of dubbing in Italy is illustrated from the advent of the first silent "talkie" in the late 1920s until the present day, in the last section the state of the art of the Italian subtitling industry is described, with a particular emphasis on the impact of changed market conditions, as well as the professional identity crisis (cf. Kapsaskis 2011).

Italy is a country where dubbing is the predominant and rather systematic form of screen translation employed, whereas subtitling is not even a secondary option on public television, being merely confined to the niche market of film festivals, DVDs and pay-TV channels.

Italy traditionally stands among those European countries labelled as "dubbing countries", along with Austria, France, Germany and Spain. In fact, geographically speaking, Europe has been ideologically divided into two groups, namely, dubbing and subtitling countries. This categorisation may appear to be oversimplified (cf. the European Commission "Study on Dubbing and Subtitling Needs and Practices in the European Audiovisual Industry" 2008), but it clearly shows to what extent other forms of audiovisual translation are eclipsed by these two practices. While, on the one hand, subtitling is typical of small countries (Netherlands, Denmark, Greece, Portugal, Belgium and Finland, for example), characterised by a small population, the presence of bilingualism and a high percentage of imported films, on the other hand, dubbing is associated with large, officially monolingual countries (Perego 2007). Yet, these features alone, do not account for the choice of dubbing as the preferred mode of translation in Italy, where historical events have played a major role.

2.1   A brief history of dubbing

The origins of Italy's strong dubbing tradition may be traced back to the 1930s. In 1927 the American film industry released *The Jazz Singer*

DOI: 10.1057/9781137470379.0006

by Alan Crosland, the first "talkie" with synchronised dialogues: though mostly silent, the film switched to "talkie mode" whenever the star, Al Jolson, was singing. The original version was first presented in Italy in 1929, causing a tidal wave of adverse reaction on the part of Mussolini's Fascist Party which responded with a ministerial decree aiming to ban the distribution of foreign films with their original soundtrack. The 1930 act stated that: "the Interior Ministry has ordered that, from today, no permission will be granted for the screening of films containing speech in a foreign language".[1]

The intervention of censorship, to counteract the predominance of American film companies and to promote the Italian cinema industry, was also meant to preserve the national language and control any information from outside the national borders perceived by the regime as inappropriate. Thus, the original film dialogues were replaced by captions, a practice that was not favourably received by the audience, as viewers were forced to make the extra effort to read while watching, and secondly because of the illiteracy rate, which in 1930, equated to 25 per cent of a population of around 40,000,000 people, with 50 per cent of people experiencing problems with reading (Di Cola 2000).

Meanwhile, American majors like MGM, Fox, and Warner Bros. in Hollywood, attempted to re-enter the Italian market by shooting multiple dubbed versions of the same film, in which actors of different nationalities would employ the same script in their mother tongue. Yet, the impediment to success of this method was that the actors – who were mainly Americans of Italian descent – used a regional dialect rather than the standard language, a feature which was perceived as phony and misleading by the receiving culture. Eventually, with the support of the fascist regime "that realised the massive appeal and impact film with sound could have on the masses" (Danan 1991: 611), the first Italian dubbing company, the Cines-Pittaluga studios based in Rome, was founded where celebrated theatre actors were recruited as dubbers, and from that moment on, the rest became history.

In time, the dubbing industry was to achieve a level of absolute excellence, despite the many drawbacks involved in the practice which do not seem to have discouraged the Italian audiovisual translation companies. Among these drawbacks, the enormous expenses and the time required for the adaptation of films may be singled out in particular. Following Danan, "in an effort to build strong nationalistic states, these countries [...] created infrastructures that are still central to their film industry

DOI: 10.1057/9781137470379.0006

today" (ibid.:611). Hence, the practice of dubbing, which was once mandatory under the pressure of the Fascist regime, not only affected the contemporary mode of transfer, but after over 80 years, it also continues to determine the preference of the audience.

Nowadays, cinema adaptors belong to a complex, uneven hierarchical structure. At the top is the elite, a small group of privileged people responsible for a large number of dubbed film versions: they decide what to translate (mainly films and high quality TV productions), and set their own, very high wages. At the bottom we find the largest group, which is made of adaptors striving for a chance to work in the film industry (Pavesi and Perego 2006). The study carried out by the authors noted above, has demonstrated that when asked about their training, adaptors affirmed that they did not believe it necessary to their profession, whereas an excellent knowledge of Italian, experience, writing skills and natural gifts seemed to be of paramount importance. Moreover, the adaptors made it clear that they did not consider themselves translators *tout-court*. Only a few of them hold a degree in translation, since professional crafts and skills are said to be acquired on the job. The manner in which adaptors join the dubbing industry is also quite revealing. Acquaintances and family relations are the key factors to success in the business, which in turn leads to an impenetrable working environment "hardly accessible to outsiders" (ibid.:105).

In recent years, Italian adaptors have been facing radical changes in the dubbing sector, "with globalisation dictating that films should be premièred simultaneously on both sides of the Atlantic" (Antonini and Chiaro 2009:99), so that a film which was once adapted in three weeks, now takes five days to be completed to the detriment of quality. Ultimately, dubbing is expensive and time-consuming; authenticity is sacrificed by depriving characters of their real voice, and most importantly, it does not seem to have adjusted to the rapid changes witnessed by the film industry in the new millennium.

2.2   The subtitling industry in Italy

In 2011, the European Commission published a study carried out by the Media Consulting Group on "Dubbing and Subtitling Needs and Practices in the European Audiovisual Industry", contained in *An Inventory of Community actions in the field of multilingualism 2011 update*,[2]

DOI: 10.1057/9781137470379.0006

and intended to encourage linguistic diversity. This document reveals that some countries traditionally inclined to dubbing (e.g., Italy, Spain and France) are progressively moving towards subtitling as far as cinema distribution is concerned, even if the costs are almost double the European average. From this study, it also emerged that, for TV broadcasters, the choice of whether to adopt dubbing or subtitling is mainly due to audience preferences. Dubbing, thus, seems a "bad habit" hard to break, since "the general public prefers the comfort of the national language" (Media Consulting Group 2008.).

The history of subtitling started with the so-called "intertitles", which first appeared in 1903 in E. S. Porter's *Uncle Tom's Cabin*, as a text inserted between the sequences of the movie. In 1938, subtitles made their debut on television when the BBC presented the first foreign film with English subtitles, Robinson's *Der Student von Prag*; yet, it was only during the 1960s that the first caption generators entered the market, and by the mid-70s the teletext system had invaded the market to such an extent that in the late 1990s "fifteen European countries were providing a teletext subtitling service for the deaf" (Ivarsson 1998:25).

Nowadays, the Italian subtitling industry mainly operates within the market for DVDs, pay-TV channels and film festivals. Following the *Subtitle Research Project*[3] – a study on the Italian subtitling industry carried out by the Department of Interdisciplinary Studies in Translation, Languages and Cultures (SITLeC), University of Bologna – the subtitling market started to develop during the 1990s with the widespread programming of DVDs and satellite channels. Accurate information about a small number of subtitling companies operating in Italy was collected as part of the study: Atlante, Classic Titles, Colby, Ellemme Edizioni, Laser Film, Microcinema, Ombre Elettriche, Raggio Verde and Underlight. Some of these companies specialise in film festivals and opera, others in cinema, with the remainder working in DVD and television subtitling (Angelucci 2004).

The first Italian subtitling company was created in the mid-80s, but it was only during the second half of the 1990s that the majority of subtitling companies entered the market. On the whole, Italian companies are relatively small with no more than 15 employees, and hire freelance professionals when necessary. The companies interviewed in the research project referred to above, agreed on the fact that the most important parameter when assessing the quality of subtitling is readability, followed by reduction, the conciseness of the subtitles and

DOI: 10.1057/9781137470379.0006

finally faithfulness to the source text. They did not seem to focus much on spotting technicalities, on translation accuracy and above all on the need to differentiate the approach to subtitling standards depending on the specific target viewers addressed (Angelucci 2004). As far as the profession is concerned, subtitlers are currently facing major challenges relating to the increasingly tight deadlines of translation projects, as well as the significantly dropping tariffs, to the extent that they cannot make a living through subtitling alone.

The European Commission has recently published a report on "The status of the translation profession in the European Union" (Pym et al. 2012), emphasising that it is, in fact, the current market disorder that has become the main focus of professional translators. Among the causes of the crisis are the declining prices, exacerbated by the widespread availability of cheap, poor quality translation, and also resulting from tight deadlines which are wholly incompatible with an adequate output, not to mention the increasingly high proportion of part-time and freelance contracts current in the translation industry as a whole. Among professionals, the vast majority of subtitlers assert that fansubbing and crowdsourcing in general are affecting the market, putting the blame on "the rise of the amateur" (O'Hagan 2011) and absolving themselves of their own guilt. It is, in fact, "the crisis of the experts who undervalue what they do not know and overvalue what they do" (Gee and Hayes, 2011:44).

Any criticism of professionals by this reference is unintentional, although it seems that they should be more aware of the changes taking place in the translation environment. According to the European report on the status of the translation profession, the changes brought about by fansubbing practices seem to have had a major impact both on translation theory and practices, not to mention on the audience's perception of subtitling (Pym et al. 2012). The study also reports that "even though crowdsourcing is still a niche activity and affects the sector only to a limited extent, its influence is bound to grow and there are useful lessons to be learnt concerning good practices for professional translators as well (ibid.:37).

Notes

1   My translation. In the original: "Il ministero dell'interno ha disposto che da oggi non venga accordato il nullaosta alla rappresentazione di pellicole

DOI: 10.1057/9781137470379.0006

cinematografiche che contengano del parlato in lingua straniera sia pure in misura minima" (Perego 2007:21).

2   A summary can be found online at: www//ec.europa.eu/culture/media/programme/docs/overview/evaluation/studies/dubbing_sub_2007/ex_sum_ds_en.pdf. date accessed 7 October 2014.

3   See more information at: www://subtitle.agregat.net/index.php/ita_open/presentation/ date accessed 20 October 2014.

DOI: 10.1057/9781137470379.0006

3

Fansubbing

Abstract: *The purpose of this chapter is to examine the phenomenon of fansubbing by monitoring the progress of amateur practices in Italy through the analysis of the philosophy of fan communities. Contemporary Italian fansubbing, relating to the subtitling-based mediation of American TV shows, constitutes the focus of this section: we have investigated the motivation behind this practice, the creation of the communities and their hierarchical structure along with the phases involved in the process, and also the technicalities needed in order to edit, produce and release the fansubs of a TV show. A description of the beliefs of ItaSA and Subsfactory is given in these sections, with an explanation of their tendency to "speak the truth" rather than to "nationalise" the dialogue for the receiving audience.*

Massidda, Serenella. *Audiovisual Translation in the Digital Age: The Italian Fansubbing Phenomenon.* Basingstoke: Palgrave Macmillan, 2015. DOI: 10.1057/9781137470379.0007.

The purpose of this chapter is to examine the phenomenon of amateur translation by monitoring the progress of fansubbing practices in Italy through the analysis of the beliefs of online communities.

Fan translation is a new "genre" within the field of audiovisual translation and has mainly been examined in connection with Japanese anime. Contemporary Italian fansubbing, relating to the subtitling-based mediation of American TV shows, constitutes the focus of this section. We have investigated the motivation behind this practice, the creation of the first online communities, their hierarchical structure and the tasks performed by fansubbers along with the various phases involved in the process, and also the technicalities needed in order to edit, produce and release the fansubbed versions of a TV programme. A description of the practices and beliefs of fansubbers is offered throughout the various sections of this chapter, with an explanation of their tendency to "speak the truth" rather than to "nationalise" the original dialogue for the receiving audience (Danan 1991).

As noted by Mangiron and O'Hagan, in fact, we will discover that "[fan translation] approaches seem to swing between reverence for the source text and the desire to remain faithful to it" (2013:302), and that the motivation behind their work is rooted both in the will to make up for the absence of official translations, and in the dissatisfaction with the poor quality of mainstream audiovisual translation.

3.1   Co-creative labour: the organised fan industry

"Amateur experts", an abstract entity created by the Web 2.0, are the "monstrous offspring" of ancient fans. Lately, much of the academic attention concerning fandom has focused on the definition of "fan" and in recent years, a large number of scholars have tackled the issue in conjunction with networked subcultures from the most disparate angles of fandom (cf. Banks & Deuze 2009; Deuze 2011; Barra &Guarnaccia 2009; Baym 2010; Boguki 2009; Bold 2012; Burwell 2010; Caffrey 2009; Casarini 2011, 2014; Chambers 2012; Chronin 2010; Díaz Cintas and Muñoz Sánchez 2006; Dwyer 2012; Fernández Costales 2011; Ferrer Simó, M. R. 2005; García 2010; Jenkins 1992, 2008; Lee 2009, 2011; Lee & Bielby 2010; Leonard 2005; Nornes 1999; O'Hagan 2008; Pérez González 2006, 2007).

As far as the etymology is concerned, the term "fan" comes from the Latin word "fanaticus", while the English derivation, "fanatic", refers to

DOI: 10.1057/9781137470379.0007

someone obsessed by an interest or enthusiasm for a particular activity (Costello and Moore 2007), thus, differentiating fans from traditional consumers since their approach to consumption is regarded as "excessive". In *Textual Poachers: Television Fans and Participatory Culture* (1992), Jenkins distinguished between "viewers" and "fans", suggesting that while viewers follow an isolated model of media consumption, far from simply consuming a product, fans participate in discussions and reflections on their experience, and are involved in a varied range of interactive activities: writing letters to producers, conversing with other fans on forums and attending fan events, for example. As a consequence, if we agree with Jenkins's definition, being a fan implies the possession of a social and cultural identity not shared by the ordinary viewer. Moreover, fans do not perceive themselves as consumers, since for them "the dichotomy between production and consumption, the supply-side and the demand-side, breaks down" (Beilby et al. 1999:37).

Over the past few decades, the widespread use of Internet technologies has virtually empowered fans, turning formerly passive media consumers into the leading actors in a major revolution, making media as co-creators and circulating user-created content incorporated into the products owned by media companies (Banks 2009). Therefore, the traditional connotation of the term "fan", as defined by Jenkins, has undergone a profound shift towards the concept of "co-creative user" (ibid.:2009). These unofficial producers have been reshaping the paradigms of the world media scenario – particularly as far as commercial television narratives are concerned – building up a force of amateur experts, that, in the case of Italy, could be regarded as a challenge to audiovisual translation practices. Díaz Cintas and Muñoz Sánchez, back in the day, saw in their activity "the seed of a new type of subtitling for the digital era" (2006:51). According to Dwyer:

> These distinctive characteristics have led many to conclude that fansubbing offers valuable lessons for professionals, not least in providing a vision of how to preserve creativity and authenticity in the face of technological change and the demands of a decentralized global mediasphere.
>
> (2012: 219)

In recent years, Italy has witnessed the emergence of a fan-based, underground form of audiovisual translation in opposition to mainstream practices. Although, the activity of fansubbers was initiated more than 20 years ago in association with Japanese anime, in the new millennium the

DOI: 10.1057/9781137470379.0007

focus has shifted towards American TV series. The project started with the most popular TV show of all time: *Lost*. The first episode of *Lost* was aired in Italy in 2005, and from that moment on, the interest surrounding this show resulted in an ever-increasing fan base. It soon developed into online communities devoted to translating the episodes into Italian, in an attempt to counteract the long waiting periods between seasons due to the fact that the dubbing process is rather a time-consuming activity. Hence, in an effort to allow fellow fans to watch their favourite TV show almost in real time with the United States, a new figure emerged on the Internet: the fansubber.

The lives of fansubbers are characterised by sleepless nights spent watching the recording of a TV episode, translating the English subtitles or even translating by ear if necessary, in order to release the Italian subtitled version as soon as possible after the episode has been aired in the USA. This revolutionary mass phenomenon has given rise to two main fansubbing communities, ItaSA and Subsfactory, producing more than a dozen "soft subs" every day. Soft subs, unlike hard subs, (which are simple text files encoded in the video stream of a TV program), are .srt files which are separate from the video clip "whose format depends on the exact subtitle encoding software to be used "[1] and loaded by users onto video players such as VideoLan Media Player that "can be turned on or off and edited based on preferences"[2] (Rembert-Lang, L. D. 2010). The choice of soft subs over hard subs, meaning that the subs are not merged with the video, is probably due to the problems relating to copyright infringement (see Chapter 1, section 3).

In addition to the reasons considered so far, Italian fansubbing communities supposedly emerged in opposition to dubbing, as a form of resistance against its supposed authenticity and the unchallenged idea that dubbing might unequivocally represent "the best of all possible worlds". While adaptation might be perceived as smooth, Italian-sounding and easily comprehensible to the average viewer, the process of domestication it undergoes does not allow for a good quality product in terms of linguistic and cultural mediation (Antonini and Chiaro 2009:100). Fansubbers and their followers perceive dubbing as an interference depriving viewers of the sense of "otherness" and leaving them with a "transnational decultured product" (Ascheid 1997:40).

In 2008, Rai4 broadcast a special edition of the programme *Sugo* devoted to the phenomenon. As explained by the amateur translators belonging to ItaSA and Subsfactory who were interviewed, their activity

DOI: 10.1057/9781137470379.0007

is aimed at "restoring" the foreign product, allowing fans to appreciate its original voices, soundtrack and atmosphere while skipping the bureaucratic delays involved before the copyright of TV shows can be acquired, the script adapted and the dialogues dubbed. The wider implications of fansubbing on audiovisual translation practices in Italy – and other dubbing countries – were clearly appreciated only four years after ItaSA and Subsfactory were created.

On 24 May 2010, a unique event took place: the final episode of *Lost* was aired simultaneously by NBC in the United States, Sky1 in the United Kingdom, Fox Italia in Italy and many more countries worldwide. In Italy the episode was aired in English at 6.00 am, and fansubbed by ItaSA and Subsfactory just a few hours later. It was then re-aired 24 hours later with Italian "pro-subtitles" and eventually broadcast on May 31 in its dubbed Italian version. Never before had Italians experienced such a speed in dealing with audiovisual translation, and it is no wonder that the "Italian fansubbing movement" paved the way for it to happen. These significant changes were discussed in an interesting forum connected to ItaSA in November 2010. In brief, the fansubbers stated that a great revolution was taking place. Concerning *Lost*, they wrote that Sky TV had dramatically reduced the traditional time lapse between seasons, managing to subtitle the show only 24 hours after the airing in the United States. All of them ultimately agreed that they had had "some hand" in it. It is, therefore, apparent that Italian amateur translators are unashamedly opinionated concerning translation matters.

Exactly who these fansubbers are is a difficult questioned to answer. The majority of them are relatively reserved, preferring to take a backseat and hiding behind nicknames. When asked about their "real life" they appear to be very evasive. However, judging from a set of online interviews conducted with the leading figures of both communities, and thanks to a collaboration with both ItaSA and Subsfactory – a three-year field research project which was spent in regular day-to-day contact with amateur translators – it can be concluded that the people who initiated this underground activity were young people between the ages of 18 and 35, belonging to a generation which had grown up in a globalised context, were linguistically aware and educated (either to an undergraduate or postgraduate level), and united by a slavish addiction to American TV shows. The founders of these communities (who allegedly collaborated for a short period of time), are best known

DOI: 10.1057/9781137470379.0007

as, e.g., Superbiagi (Subsfactory) and Klonni (ItaSA), very well-known nicknames to the adherents of fansubbing.

3.2   Origins of ItaSA and Subsfactory

In the previous sections we have described how in the new millennium, the focus of fansubbing shifted in favour of American TV series. After an initial outline of the Italian fansubbing phenomenon, the coordinating mechanism underlying the two major online communities, ItaSA and Subsfactory, are introduced.

ItaSA was created in 2005, in the wake of the exceptional interest aroused by *Lost*. It is a large community of fansubbers, much larger than Subsfactory, more popular and "younger", with staff members aged between 16 and 30, with end-user in the same age group. The latter, Subsfactory, is the first Italian fansubbing community – its genesis as a fan base dating back to the 1990s, when a small group of fans started to translate sci-fi TV series gravitating around the world of *Star Trek* – although their website was, in fact, created much later in 2005.

Subsfactory is smaller, "older" – subbers are aged between 17 and 60 – and less popular than ItaSA, even though it has recently been gaining increasing success, thanks to the widespread use of social networking sites, such as Facebook and Twitter. Although there are rumours to the effect that they collaborated for a short while in 2006, these communities currently occupy the opposite ends of the spectrum. Apart from the fact that they hold different views on translation – Subsfactory claims to be more faithful to the source text and ItaSA admits to leaving more space for the creativity of the subber (Barra and Guarnaccia 2009) – they also differ concerning their main starting point, with ItaSA aiming to "get there first", releasing the subs as soon as possible after the airing of the American TV show, while Subsfactory proudly claims to give priority to accuracy rather than speed (ibid:2009). There is evidently an intense rivalry as well as more positive spirit of competition between the two communities, pushing them towards high levels of performance.

Contrary to expectations, new fan entities are entering the arena: in the last few years, Italy has witnessed the rise of collective subphenomena derived from the founding fathers of fansubbing: for example, Angels and Demons,[3] Myitsubs,[4] Nowaysubs,[5] Subsfamily[6] and Subspedia.[7]

DOI: 10.1057/9781137470379.0007

What these newly formed groups have in common is a frenetic desire to release their fansubs as fast as possible. As a result, they do whatever is in their power to meet their needs with regard to TV shows. Engaged in a sort of "to the last breath" competition, they produce amateur subtitles a fast as they possibly can to the detriment of translation quality. This second wave of Italian fansubbers (probably emerged following what we would define as a "spore-effect" process in which would-be fansubbers rejected by either ItaSA or Subsfactory after a probationary period went on to form less demanding and more accessible fansubbing entities) finished up by disgracing Italian fan translation. Everything that has being said about fansubbing ethics so far seems somewhat meaningless when applied to these groups: fansubbing values, rooted in accuracy, faithfulness and strict adherence to the source text, have been marginalised to the point where the translations produced by the new communities show a total misunderstanding of the scriptwriters' intentions resulting in mistranslations characterised by major grammatical, lexical and morphological errors as far as Italian is concerned. Nevertheless, the majority of fans seem unaware of these widespread mistakes and are more than glad to access their favourite TV shows as soon as possible even if the final and fairly mediocre output is more of a nuisance than a pleasure.

Metaphorically speaking, it is as if they were attempting to illuminate a room by lighting a match. Indeed, a fit for purpose, slapdash translation can only convey a very confused and vague idea of the original dialogue. It is to be hoped that this might just represent a primitive stage and that it will be followed by an adjustment to the traditional path already traced by ItaSA and Subsfactory.

3.3   The fansubbing machine

> *"This well-oiled machine made of standard routines*
> *closely mirrors professional companies practices.*
> *Yet, fansubbing communities are no-profit groups*
> *solely driven by personal motivation,*
> *a flare for sharing and maybe*
> *a little bit of narcissism."*[8]

(Barra and Guarnaccia 2009:2)

Given the enormous commitment in terms of hours, the activities of fansubbers resemble a job more than a hobby. The "fansubbing factory"

DOI: 10.1057/9781137470379.0007

can be likened to a strategic pyramid-shaped structure, made of progressive hierarchical subdivisions in terms of tasks. These unofficial workers are organised into teams committed to the translation of a specific TV show, and coordinated by an appointed reviser. Before the episode is even aired in the United States, the reviser makes sure the team is ready and available for the forthcoming task. Upon confirmation, the team starts the operating machine, first searching for both the original video and the .ts raw online.[9]

As a matter of fact, subbers employ readymade English subtitles originating from Chinese sources, rather than translating by ear, which they do more rarely. Sometimes, when these resources are not available, they may rely on transcripts obtained either via OCR or voice recognition software.[10] Once retrieved, the English subtitle file is uploaded in a private area of the forum together with the reviser's subdivision of tasks and the final deadline. Thus, subbers may choose to work directly on the .srt file, which is converted into a .txt file or to use some open source software for different OS[11] such as Subtitle Workshop and Visual SubSynch (Windows), Subtitle Editor (Linux) or Miyu and Jubler (Mac OS X), to name but a few. Subsequently, subbers – also fulfilling the role of "synchers"[12] – start the cueing phase in order to adjust the "in" and "out" of subtitles in perfect harmony with both the soundtrack and the images. Amateur experts do not work alone. Throughout the process, they operate as a collaborative team, supporting each other by communicating through specific threads on the forum or via IM in real time. Moreover, a set of established guidelines (see Chapter 4 for an insight on fansubbing conventions) assist fansubbers to standardise the terminology, the number of characters and the cps[13] allowed for each subtitle, the editing and formatting standards, the punctuation conventions, the use of accents and so on. When the Italian version is ready, each subber submits his/her own part to the reviser who collects the files merging them in order to finalise the process. During this phase, the emphasis is on linguistic and technical revision, and particularly on translation consistency and fluency. The .srt file is then released and uploaded online to a dedicated repository ready to be shared by the whole virtual community.

ItaSA and Subsfactory are also open to new members eager to contribute to the cause. Would-be translators are "hired" upon completion of an entrance test. They are given a zipped folder containing an .avi file and an .srt file to be uploaded in Subtitle Workshop. More often than not,

DOI: 10.1057/9781137470379.0007

the subtitles in question may be in a different language from the original soundtrack (e.g. Portuguese rather than English) and the ripped video may belong to an unknown TV show. These combined factors may ultimately result in a challenging task for aspiring fansubbers (see Chapter 4, section 3 for an insight on the roles of fansubbers in the communities).

Notes

1 Anime Mikome, *What is a Fansub? Hardsubs and Softsubs*, http://anime.mikomi.org/wiki/WhatIsFansub.
2 Bloomsburg University Manga and Anime Club, Fansub, www.bumac.org/index.php?page=fansub.
3 www.italiansubtitles.blogspot.it.
4 http://myitsubtitles.weebly.com.
5 http://nowaysubs.blogfree.net.
6 http://subsfamily-subs.weebly.com.
7 http://subspedia.weebly.com.
8 My translation. In the original: ".[...] una macchina oliata, con routine produttive ormai standard, con una divisione del lavoro [...] con una scala gerarchica interiorizzata dai componenti del gruppo, con un'organizzazione che non lascia nulla al caso. Come – e più – che in un'azienda. Solo che qui non ci sono fini di lucro: a far girare ogni ingranaggio sono[...] la gratuità del dono e un po' di narcisismo".
9 The "ts" (MPEG transport stream) is obtained by exporting and converting the closed captions displayed on TV into a suitable format.
10 Optical character recognition software programmes allow the conversion of scanned PDF files into editable Word documents.
11 Operating systems.
12 The role of the subber and the "syncher" may be played by the same person. This is the case of Subsfactory's "master subber", able to translate and also spot or "synch" their subtitles.
13 Characters per Second.

DOI: 10.1057/9781137470379.0007

4
Subtitling and Fansubbing Standards: A Hybrid Proposal

Abstract: *The first section of this chapter opens with an introduction to the main features of subtitling and closes with a brief overview of standard subtitling practices. The codes of practice used by fansubbers are explored in the second section and a comprehensive description of the fansubbing guidelines used both by ItaSA and Subsfactory is given. In this section, which includes an analysis of the different treatment of punctuation conventions in professional subtitling and fansubbing, the topic of translation norms is dealt with fairly extensively. A definition of the theoretical approach followed is offered in the final section in order to advance a hybrid proposal for future subtitling norms, following an analysis of the standards used by both professional and amateur subtitlers.*

Massidda, Serenella. *Audiovisual Translation in the Digital Age: The Italian Fansubbing Phenomenon.* Basingstoke: Palgrave Macmillan, 2015. DOI: 10.1057/9781137470379.0008.

DOI: 10.1057/9781137470379.0008

The first section of this chapter opens with an introduction to the main features of subtitling and closes with a brief overview of standard subtitling practices. The codes of practice used by fansubbers are explored in the second section and a comprehensive description of the fansubbing guidelines used both by ItaSA and Subsfactory is given. In this chapter, which includes an analysis of the different treatment of punctuation conventions in professional subtitling and fansubbing, the topic of translation norms is dealt with fairly extensively. A definition of the theoretical approach followed is offered in the final section in order to advance a hybrid proposal for future subtitling norms, following an analysis of the standards used by both professional and amateur subtitlers.

4.1   General standards in professional subtitling

In this section a brief overview of mainstream subtitling features and practices is given, based on previous studies carried out by a number of academics (cf. Luyken et al., 1991; Ivarsson, 1992; Gottlieb, 1998; Ivarsson and Carroll, 1998; Kovacic, 1991; De Linde and Kay 1999; Díaz Cintas, 2001 and 2003; Chaume, 2004; Díaz Cintas and Remael, 2007; Georgakopoulou, 2003).

According to De Linde and Kay, "the main condition of subtitling stems from the integration of text, sound and image, the reading capabilities of target viewers, and the restrictions which these two factors place on space and time" (1999:6). This definition is a clever attempt at condensing a variety of fundamental traits characteristic of subtitling into a few lines. Audiovisual translation in general, and subtitling in particular, represents a constrained form of translation characterised by a shift of mode from speech to writing, where the message is conveyed by both the aural and visual channels within several spatio-temporal limitations. Linguistically speaking, two main different types of subtitling may be distinguished:

1   Intralingual subtitling, or same-language subtitling, for the deaf and hard of hearing (SDH or either HoH);
2   Interlingual subtitling which implies the translation of one language into another.

The second category is the focus of this chapter, provided in an attempt to list the stages involved in the process of subtitling. The first stage involves

DOI: 10.1057/9781137470379.0008

the so-called "timing", "spotting" or "cueing" process. Depending on the subtitling company, the practice of setting the "in" and "out" of subtitles can be performed either by specific technicians, or by the subtitlers them-selves. Unfortunately, as far as freelance professionals are concerned, the current trend is to provide them with pre-established time codes or "templates". The next phase focuses on the translation of the original dialogue, followed by the editing process along with the segmentation of subtitles based on semantic-syntactic criteria, and then the final revision carried out by the subtitler. These are the main stages involved in a proc-ess governed by the long-established and almost unanimously accepted rules cursorily described in the next section.

4.2   Subtitling codes of conduct

Subtitling is a well-established form of constrained audiovisual transla-tion. Many scholars have argued that it is closer to the process of adapta-tion (Delabastita 1989) than to translation *tout court*. It is characterised by specific communicative purposes and by the use of standard norms aimed to simplify the source text in order to facilitate the interpreta-tion of the original message (Perego 2007). Among the various features characteristic of subtitling, one in particular makes it unique: both the source and target texts co-exist on screen, enabling viewers to hear the original soundtrack and read the subtitles at the same time. As a result, subtitling is exposed to all sort of criticism on the part of viewers who, depending on their linguistic competence, may find fault with if it does not match what they hear, thus considering it unreliable. In addi-tion, another relevant aspect of this mode of transfer is "the filtering of potential loss of information" (Tveit 2009:21), since the written channel does not allow for the nuances of speech to be accurately conveyed: "the written words cannot possibly compete with speech" (ibid:21). What is more, converting spoken language into written text often leads to the use of "nominalisation" strategies in Italian, a transformation that prevents subtitles from retaining the naturalness and orality typical of spontane-ous speech. Yet, despite the almost inevitable loss of linguistic nuances implied in the "diamesic shift" from the oral to the written mode (Perego 2007), good subtitles are supposed to pass unnoticed and act as guidance throughout the viewing experience.

DOI: 10.1057/9781137470379.0008

As Minchinton puts it, viewers just "blink down at the subtitles for information, they 'photograph' them rather than read them" (1993:14–15). With regard to reading speed, the issue becomes extremely complicated since, as Díaz-Cintas puts it: .

> The amount of information we can write on any given subtitle will depend on the assumed reading speed of our target viewers. Since the audience is potentially very diverse in [...] age and educational background, it is [...] rather difficult to agree on a reading speed that is adequate for all viewers.
>
> (2008:96–97)

He further explains that the "six-second-rule", traditionally employed in TV subtitling, in which a two-liner containing 37 characters per line can be comfortably read in six seconds by the average viewer, ultimately results in "12 subtitling characters per second (cps) or 140–150 words per minute (wpm)" (ibid.:97). These calculations date back to the 1980s, however, and are thus fairly outdated by comparison with current standards. In addition, digital technology, now based on pixels, "has made it easier [...] to move from characters to proportional lettering, which allows for [more] space available" (ibid.:97). This shift to proportional lettering has made it possible to maximise the use of space in subtitling terms: the letter "i" occupies less space than the letter "o" in a word, for example.

Technically speaking, in fact, subtitling presents translators with two constraining factors, space and time, profoundly affecting the way subtitles appear on screen. Subtitles may be displayed with a maximum of two lines – with an average of 37/40 characters per line (depending on the subtitling company) in the case of Italian – and their exposure time ranges between one and six seconds, the ideal span of time allowing the viewer to read at an appropriate speed (Luyken et al. 1991). Furthermore, following Díaz-Cintas and Remael, subtitles should be "semantically and syntactically self-contained" (2007:172), since good quality and coherent line breaks are supposed to facilitate readability and comprehension on the part of the viewer. Ideally, in the case of two-line subtitles, the first line should be shorter than the second. Needless to say, this is not always feasible, as segmentation is a relatively difficult art. Priority should always be given to the completeness of meaning within each line of the subtitle, while the aesthetic norm noted above is only a secondary consideration. Due to the limited time and space available for the subtitles, linguistic limitations may be dealt with by employing the strategy of "reduction".

DOI: 10.1057/9781137470379.0008

According to Kovačič's categorisation, we can distinguish among three levels of discourse elements: "the indispensable, the partly dispensable and the dispensable" (1991:409). While the indispensable elements are essential and must be translated in order to convey the crucial information contained in the original dialogue and also for the audience to follow the plot of a film, the partly dispensable can be condensed, and the dispensable elements can be simply omitted. As a result, subtitlers usually leave out some words that are universally known ("yes" and "no", for instance), repetitions, utterances conveying a phatic function ("well" and "you know", for example), false starts and exclamations that do not need a translation as they are easily understandable by viewers all round the world.

The "relevance theory", as proposed by Sperber and Wilson (1986), might constitute an interesting approach to dealing with the strategy of reduction in subtitling. According to this theory, "an assumption is relevant in a context if, and only if, it has some contextual effect in the context" (Sperber and Wilson 1995:122). As a result, subtitlers should aim to express similar "contextual effects of an utterance in a given context" (Kovačič 1994:247). Unfortunately, this is not always feasible, owing to the complexity of segmentation. Although it is true that the subtitled version of a programme is always a condensed form of the source dialogue, "it is too limited to view subtitling as a mere condensation of a so-called original" (Gambier, Shlesinger, and Stolze 2007:278). As the authors of *Doubts and Directions in Translation Studies* explain, when analysing a subtitled version of an audiovisual product, the perception of a variety of omissions and a difference in the number of words transferred from one language to another occurs fairly naturally, although what really matters are not these losses or additions, the focal point being "what is transformed and why" (ibid.:278). Hence, in the creation of interlingual subtitles, the strategy of "condensation" and "relevance theory" should always be balanced with the notion of equivalence.

Kruger (2001) has attempted to investigate this relationship by using the semiotic approach as a starting point. In her opinion, semiotics, or "the study of signs and sign-using behavior", and "interpretative semiotics" in particular, seem to explain this delicate balance. According to this theory, three categories of equivalence, the "qualitative", the "referential" and the "significational" are identified (Gorlée 1994). While "qualitative equivalence" refers to the external features of the sign (rhyme structure, for example), "referential equivalence" refers both to the "immediate

DOI: 10.1057/9781137470379.0008

object" of a sign, or "the idea called up directly by a particular sign use" (ibid.:176) and the "dynamical object", that is "the hypothetical sum of all instances of the sign-bound immediate object" (ibid.:177). "Significational equivalence", instead, refers to the relationship between the object and the "interpretant", considered as "that which the sign produces in the quasi-mind which is the interpreter" (Eco 1976:68). In Kruger's opinion, the latter is apparently the only type of equivalence to ensure that the effect produced by the text in the source language viewers is similar to the perception of the translated text in the target language viewers. According to Kruger's perspective, subtitlers can "deviate" from the source text by producing "a new target text which is nevertheless significationally equivalent to the original" (Kruger 2001:185).

In 1998 Carroll and Ivarsson presented a proposal for good subtitling practices[1] endorsed by the European Association for Studies in Screen Translation (ESIST). This comprehensive document covers both translation and time coding practices, so that its use is felt to be appropriate here, since it constitutes a standard example. It is summarised as follows.

Regarding translation, subtitlers should:

1 work on a dialogue list along with a glossary of specific terminology and special references;
2 focus on high-quality translation, paying attention to cultural nuances, appropriate register and correct grammar;
3 use simple syntactic units distributed on a maximum of two lines;
4 distribute the text in syntactically self-contained subtitles, (if on a two-liner subtitle the length is unequal, the upper line should be shorter in order to reduce eye movement);
5 avoid repetitions of names and common expressions;

As far spotting is concerned, subtitlers should:

1 follow the rhythm of the dialogues, taking into consideration shot changes and sound bridges;
2 pay attention to those elements in dialogue that convey suspense and surprise when cueing the subtitles;
3 follow the seven-second rule[2] (min. 1, max. 7 second per subtitle), and respect the maximum cps (number of characters per second, around 70 in 6 seconds), in order to facilitate the readability of the message;
4 leave at least four frames between subtitles enabling to perceive the shift from one subtitle to the next.

DOI: 10.1057/9781137470379.0008

During the translation phase, subtitlers are faced with a variety of challenges imposed by spatio-temporal limitations; these may be overcome by adopting a range of strategies, for example text reduction and omission (partial and total), condensation (at word/close level) and reformulation, which should always sound idiomatic and fluent in the target language (Díaz Cintas and Remael, 2007).

This brief overview of interlingual subtitling is not intended to be exhaustive. It is intended to provide a general introduction to subtitling, as it represents a starting point from which to develop a more specific investigation concerning the differences between the professional and amateur subtitling guidelines.

4.3   Fansubbing guidelines

This section, which is intended to provide information on fansubbing practices, is based on a three-year field research project spent as a member of the two communities under analysis, and hence in regular day-to-day contact with amateur translators belonging to both ItaSA and Subsfactory.

In order to understand fully how the fansubbing machine works, its guidelines will be analysed.

Both communities under analysis, ItaSA and Subsfactory, present fansubbers with a set of guidelines to be followed during the translation process. The list includes a variety of information concerning each step of the process, from the spotting to the editing of the subtitles. ItaSA's guidelines will be analysed first of all, and a description of the organisation of their workflow as shown on their website will be given. Subsequently, Subsfactory's standards and practices, their approaches to translation and subtitling synchronisation will be presented, with a list of rules, tips and tricks of the trade.

4.3.1   The ItaSA method

The first community to be analysed here is ItaSA, a large community created in 2005 and composed of fansubbers aged between 16 and 30 years old, with end-users belonging to the same age group. When ItaSA was first approached, an analysis of the homepage of their website (www.italiansubs) and their forum was the first task. On a

DOI: 10.1057/9781137470379.0008

private translation area of the forum ("pannello Itasiano"), *junior translators* can access: on the left, a list of notifications of the fansubs that have just been submitted, and on the right a list of teams to which the fansubber in question belongs. A list of TV genres translated is followed by another table displaying the details relating to the specific episode, being accessed under "traduzioni" ("translations"), namely the deadline ("scadenza"), the TV show genre, the "status" – team available or unavailable – the number of fansubbers needed ("posti") and the name of the reviser ("revisore") appointed for the translation of the programme. The workflow seems very well-organised and professional for a group of unpaid and untrained translators which has currently reached almost 500 members. The roles of the ItaSA fan experts within the community are summarised in the following table (Figure 4.1).

Among the translators we find "junior translators", the new would-be fansubbers, the ones who have passed the entry test and must demonstrate their skills to the community; "translators" (qualified fansubbers who have passed the trial period) and "senior translators", the subbers who have been promoted to the role of "revisers" (proofreaders and coordinators) after a certain period of time spent in the fan group. "Resynchers", also listed among the various roles covered, are responsible for adjusting the spotting in the fansubbed version to accord with the various versions available online.[3] There are also "synchmasters", who are responsible for teaching would-be translators the art of timing, and finally the "administrators" who take care of the website and "run" the fansubbing company.[4] Having described the main roles in the fansubbing

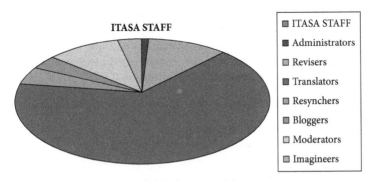

FIGURE 4.1   *Average figures referred to October 2014 (500 members)*

DOI: 10.1057/9781137470379.0008

machine, therefore, we should, now turn to an analysis of the fansubbers' guidelines, focusing on the different approaches differentiating them from professional subtitling norms. ItaSA's "Vademecum for Translators" covers the following points:

1 Software programmes employed
Jubler, Miyu, Subtitle Editor, Subtitle Workshop, Visual Sub Sync [ItaSA Mod].
2 Translation norms
  ▸ 45 characters per line, on maximum two lines (90 characters);
  ▸ duration: between 1–5 seconds (one second for monosyllables or two very short words;
  ▸ never reach the five seconds, and always keep it lower;
  ▸ italics for flashbacks and songs (adding the hash [#] symbol);
  ▸ apostrophes instead of diacritics (since video players cannot "read" them): à, è, ì, ù, ò, become a', e', i', o', u';
  ▸ asterisks for doubts regarding translation renderings;
  ▸ standard format for the file to be submitted: Title + episode + nickname + part:
  ▸ example, LilBush.1x04.Boby.126–257.

4.3.2 Subsfactory's modus operandi

The following guidelines outline Subsfactory's standards for fansubbing. In contrast to ItaSA's, their "Guida del Traduttore" ("guide for translators") is much longer and more detailed.

Its incipit, which is addressed to future fansubbers, states that:

> The guide you will read is the result of years spent translating, of discussions between subbers and revisers. It is a sort of vademecum for your very first translation and contains the main Italian grammar rules. Reading the guide is not optional, on the contrary, it is compulsory for everyone, since each translation must follow the established conventions.[5]

Here is a resume of fansubbers' rules, tips and tricks of the trade:

1 Software programmes employed
Jubler, Media Subtitler, Subtitle Workshop, Visual Sub Sync.
2 Translation norms
  ▸ Maximum two lines of no more than 45 characters each.

DOI: 10.1057/9781137470379.0008

▸ Make the lines even, divide up the text into whole sentences and avoid subtitles like the following:

> example: I ain't saying he shouldn't. I wasn't told to
> invite him.

The following would be better:

> example: I ain't saying he shouldn't.
> I wasn't told to invite him.

▸ Apostrophes instead of diacritics (since video players cannot "read" them):

> à, è, ì, ù, ò, become a', e', i', o', u'.

3   Timing

A list of norms follows on after a set of technical instructions on how to use various types of subtitling software (113 pages):

▸ 1–6 seconds allowed for each subtitle.

▸ Subtitles expressing humour, suspense and surprise should be treated carefully: never anticipate a piece of information (e.g., punch lines) placing it before the speaker actually utters the sentence containing it.

▸ Remember to cue text from letters, signs, newspapers and so on.

4   Tips

▸ First of all, watch the whole episode (with English subtitles or the "ts" provided).

▸ Synch your part before translating, then edit your subtitles and finally translate.

▸ Avoid calques; remember that the structure of Italian sentences is different from English ones.

▸ Once revised and uploaded on the website, check your translation and read the feedback written by your reviser in order to learn from your mistakes.

Subsequently, a list of online resources and glossaries specific to each TV show translated by the community is included. Subsfactory is smaller than ItaSA – 201versus 500 members (cf. Tables 4.1 and 4.2) – yet judging by their guidelines, they appear to be more accurate and rigorous as far as translation and timing are concerned.

In addition, fansubbers and fans belonging to the community often reflect on their work in various topics found on their forum. Some of them discuss the difference between professional and amateur subtitles and what emerges from these exchanges is that the majority of fans find

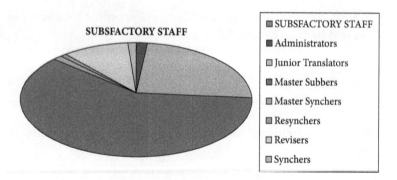

FIGURE 4.2   *Average figures referred to October 2014 (201 members)*

fault with the extreme conciseness of mainstream subtitles – "ridotti all'osso", literally reporting what they wrote, or "cut down to the bone" – since they seem to convey only the gist of original dialogues, leaving out their stylistic flavour and play on words. They also believe that subtitles are not meant to facilitate the viewer's experience of a foreign product, but that they should be in tune with the specific audience requirements concerning faithfulness and accuracy. They believe that the translation of TV shows should be treated more carefully, given the "serialised format" which tends to develop a very distinctive inside talk throughout the seasons. As a consequence, mainstream subtitling is thus perceived as extremely irritating and condescending so that fansubbers feel betrayed and treated like half-wits who are unable to perceive both the visual and the written codes at the same time. Amateur translators and their followers are the most proficient target audience regarding subtitling, so that it might be appropriate to differentiate between them and the average viewer in terms of characters per line and reading speed standards. Overall, they agree on the fact that the ability to read subtitles is just a question of training: the more you watch subtitled products, the more proficient you become.

Figure 4.2 shows the roles of the members of Subsfactory within the community. A distinction is made between "junior translators" (Subber in prova or S.I.P, provisional subbers), the equivalent of the would-be translator, and "master subbers" who have passed the entry test and are able to translate and cue subtitles; "revisers" who act as proofreaders and coordinators. "Resynchers", also listed among the various roles covered, are responsible for adjusting the spotting in the fansubbed version to accord with the various versions available online. There are also "synch-masters", who are responsible for teaching would-be translators the art of timing and finally the site administrators.

Having examined the practices of both communities, we might conclude that a greater number of characters allowed per line is among the most distinctive features of fansubbing, when compared to the reduced freedom characteristic of professional subtitling. It may be argued that fansubs are aesthetically cumbersome, yet there are some positive aspects. Subbers are left with more space available in order to express the necessary nuances in the source language dialogue – for example the reproduction of an adequate style and register – aspects that are systematically cut out in professional subtitling. What is more, what some scholars simply define as "literal translation" or "traduzione-specchio" (Bruti & Zanotti 2012), it is not a naive trait: fansubbers work on the "ts", a file obtained by converting the closed captions on TV and intended to serve the needs of viewers with an aural impairment. SDH, or subtitling for the deaf and hard of hearing, often employs "verbatim captions" rendered in the form of a literal and faithful transcription of the dialogue list, and not as a form of edited captions, condensed and simplified. Hence, in a way, we can state that fansubbing practices are driven and influenced by SDH norms. Moreover, fansubbers rarely employ the 45 character line, and only when the cps allow it. The user-friendly guide suggests that, should the lines translated exceed the 45 characters limit, the subtitling software will be automatically set to solve the problem by splitting the line, or to produce two perfectly symmetrical lines. In accordance with professional subtitling norms, semantic segmentation is paramount in fansubbing. In fact, subbers are strongly advised to produce self-contained lines. A long list of false friends and common mistakes with regard to punctuation are also included in the fansubbing guidelines, for example, the use of capital letters after an ellipsis, the different uses of punctuation in English and Italian, and above all, the correct use of diacritical marks and apostrophes. As already mentioned in this section, apart from the freedom derived from the 45 permissible characters per line, the paramount feature of "abusive subtitling" (Nornes 1999) is the "source-oriented" approach to translation, a topic which will be examined in the following sections, which are devoted respectively to the eye tracking system and the issue of audience reception, and to the "hybrid proposal" posited in the opening of this chapter.

DOI: 10.1057/9781137470379.0008

4.4   Audience reception: the eye tracking system

Before introducing the hybrid proposal, it would seem appropriate to mention briefly the issue of the audience reception of non-professional subtitling as a way of understanding whether the hybrid proposal could conceivably constitute a viable option. We would, therefore, like to refer to the pilot studies carried out by Orrego-Carmona (2014a; 2014b), Perego (2010) and Caffrey (2009) employing the eye tracking system in order to investigate this largely under-researched topic. The eye tracker (a technological device used to measure the movement or the point of fixation of the eye when viewing video images) is a system borrowed from other research fields, namely, cognitive linguistics and psychology and applied to audience reception studies for the first time by the Belgian team supervised by Géry d'Ydewalle (cf. d'Ydewalle, Van Rensbergen and Pollet 1987; d'Ydewalle and Gielen 1992; d'Ydewalle & Pavakanun 1997; d'Ydewalle, Praet, Verfaille & Van Rensbergen 1991).

In 2014, Orrego-Carmona conducted an experiment on nine students. They were asked to watch a 103-second excerpt from the TV series *The Big Bang Theory* with "pro-am" (Leadbeater and Miller 2004), or "professional-amateur" subtitles, "guided by the principle of producing subtitles that are at a near-professional quality level" (Orrego-Carmona 2014a:2), innovative subtitles, that "explore new possibilities [...] such as variations in terms of colours and fonts, creative spelling to express emotions [and also including] surtitles or glosses to add supplementary information" (ibid.:2) and professional subtitles. The results from the eye-tracking data demonstrate that, first of all, the audience reception depends on the students' level of English. It was felt that they would demonstrate "a greater degree of comprehension with professional subtitling [even though] their level of satisfaction with [...] the translation does not vary significantly" (ibid.:1). Yet, as the author himself suggests, the methodology employed should be further implemented since a larger sample of participants is needed in order to provide more reliable data.

The second case study carried out on audience reception includes both the PhD research project conducted by Caffrey (2009) and the experiment carried out by Perego (2010) both focusing on the application of the eye tracker to the viewing of Japanese anime in order to understand the impact of "pop-up glosses", which are represented by notes in the form of speech bubbles positioned at the top of the screen, that "appear and disappear together with the subtitles [...] making their reading rather

DOI: 10.1057/9781137470379.0008

challenging" (Díaz Cintas and Muñoz Sánchez 2006:10). Both studies revealed that when pop-up glosses appeared on screen, the audience perceived the subtitles as "faster" (with a higher reading speed), thus finding it fairly difficult to read, because they were forced to make an effort in order to process the information represented by the glosses in addition to the subtitles.

We are of the opinion that, while the eye tracking system might represent a useful tool in order to measure the audience reception of amateur subtitles, as revealed by Orrego-Carmona's study, this system could not possibly represent a benchmark able to reveal once and for all how intrusive subtitles are generally perceived to be by the viewers. In fact, we have noted fairly extensively in this book, that a study addressed to a single, monolithic audience may finish up by being totally unreliable, since in the case of fan translation, researchers have to deal with compartmental niche audiences with different needs, as well as diverse linguistic and cultural competences.

4.5   A hybrid proposal

> "There is a potential and emerging subtitling practice
> that accounts for the unavoidable limits in time and space
> of the subtitle, a practice that does not feign completeness,
> that does not hide its presence through restrictive rules."
>
> (Nornes 1999:13)

The issue of translation norms has attracted the interest of researchers over the past few decades (cf. Carroll 2004; Chesterman 1993, 1997, 1998; Georgakopoulou, 2003; Hermans 1991, 1996, 1999; Ivarsson, 1992; Ivarsson and Carroll 1998; Karamitroglou 1998, 2000; Nord, 1991, 1997; Pedersen 2011; Pym, Shlesinger & Simeoni 2008; Toury 1980). These norms will be analysed in the present chapter from the perspective of Toury's Descriptive Translation Studies (1995). In other words, the evolution of subtitling conventions as a result of the empirical observation of translational behaviour (Pedersen 2011) will be examined. Since there is no unanimous consensus of opinion as far as the term "norm" is concerned, Chesterman's concept of "expectancy and operational norms" (1997) will be referred to here, understood in the sense that, while "expectancy norms" indicate the audience's expectations of subtitled products, "professional norms" refer to the universally accepted

DOI: 10.1057/9781137470379.0008

rules followed by translators (cf. Sokoli 2011:21–27). For a more detailed insight into the theoretical and methodological approaches employed in this book, see the sections devoted to "context and methodology" and "reflections on theory" in the opening of the monograph.

In his 1998 paper, "A Proposed Set of Subtitling Standards in Europe", Karamitroglou has attempted to classify a series of subtitling standards enabling European countries to operate as a single unit. He argues that, although the sudden departure from long-established conventions might seem difficult at first, the introduction of minor changes to these established norms could be gradually accepted over time. Despite the challenge involved in keeping up with the very latest developments and cultural trends, production companies, customers commissioning the subtitles and professional translators, should all make an effort to adapt to this constant process of social and technological transformations (Hermans 1999).

The subtitling conventions covered by Karamitroglou (1998) are analysed below:

1   General aim
    Facilitate access to audiovisual products by favouring the readability of the subtitles produced.

2   Layout
    Subtitles, which are positioned on the lower part of the screen, should be displayed on a maximum of two lines with around 35 characters per line (40 characters would reduce the readability); the font colour should be white.

3   Duration
    The average reading speed (viewers aged from 14 to 65, from an upper-middle socio-educational class) ranges between 150–180 words per minute (between 2.5–3 words per second).

4   Segmentation
    In a two-liner each subtitle should display a semantically self-contained sentence, "as equal in length as possible, since the [...] eye is more accustomed to reading text in a rectangular rather than a triangular format." (ibid. 1998:1).

5   Omission
    Translators are not requested to transfer everything, "even when this is spatio-temporally feasible" (ibid. 1998:1). As a consequence,

DOI: 10.1057/9781137470379.0008

the elements that are classified as irrelevant are normally sacrificed in subtitling, including false starts, redundant words (repetitions, indicators of politeness), discourse markers (for example, "well", "so", "but"), down-toners and intensifiers ("nearly", "almost", "utterly" and "really", for example). However, sometimes, these apparently nonessential features have the valuable function of conveying both characterisation and the style of an audiovisual product (for further details, see the case studies analysed in Chapter 5).

By using Karamitroglou's codes of practice as a benchmark, it is possible to single out the main deviations detected in the translational behaviour of fansubbers. Concerning their general aims, subbers belonging to both ItaSA and Subsfactory, state that the main purpose of their translations is faithfulness to the source text within the set of spatio-temporal constraints that allows for up to 45 characters per line (a limit seldom reached). As far as reading speed, punctuation and segmentation parameters are concerned, amateur practices are almost identical to professional ones. Conversely, the topic of omission is treated rather differently. Subbers aim to convey "everything" belonging to the original dialogues, deeming it of paramount importance to detach themselves from the mainstream practices of "domestication" and the excessive conciseness of professional subtitling, while, "moving the viewer towards the movie", to paraphrase a well-known assertion made by Schleiermacher in 1813 (Lefevere 1977:74).

The majority of subtitling manuals suggest that perfect subtitles should pass unnoticed and guide the spectator through the viewing experience by minimising any graphical "disturbance". As a consequence, after being suitably adapted to the receiving culture, they should flow naturally as if written in the local tongue. Yet, in 1999, prior to the Italian fansubbing phenomenon, Nornes argued that it was time to rethink audiovisual modes of translation, given the significant function played by multiculturalism and diversity in our societies. Since the new millennium, which was characterised by major technological breakthroughs, and with the advent of Web 2.0, a factor that dramatically altered the essentially passive role of consumers concerning audiovisual goods, following the same routines has proved to be unacceptable. Seen in this light, what professional subtitlers discard a priori as a textual and graphic violation, may end up constituting a new experimental field in translation. This is fansubbing's major contribution to translation studies.

DOI: 10.1057/9781137470379.0008

The first scholar to have introduced the concept of "abusive transla-tion" was Lewis in 1985. His post-structuralist approach sheds light on current fansubbing norms, highlighting the fact that translation should represent an accurate interpretation of the source text, even if the adop-tion of a source-oriented approach may lead to profound alterations of the syntactic and structural boundaries imposed by the target language. Venuti clearly described the task of "abusive subtitlers" by quoting Nornes in *The Translation Studies Reader*:

> The abusive subtitler assumes a respectful stance vis-à-vis the original text, tampering with both language and the subtitling apparatus itself" so as to signal the linguistic and cultural differences of the foreign film. He imagines a range of experimental procedures that include different styles of the trans-lating language to match the stylistic peculiarities of the screenplay, as well as changes in the font, colour, and positioning of the subtitles to complement the visual and aural qualities of the film.
>
> (Venuti, 2004:332)

More recently, Caffrey (2009) has pointed out that the advent of Web 2.0 has had a major influence on the development of co-creative online communities, allowing untrained and amateur subtitlers to translate and share "abusive subtitles" that break free from professional graph-ics and linguistic norms in order to produce a more transparent and authentic translation. Abusive subtitling appears to challenge the "corrupt" mainstream procedures which obscure the original from its end-viewers (Nornes 2004). While Jenkins (1992) was the first academic to perceive amateur practices as a form of resistance to the media industry, Nornes was the first scholar to define mainstream standards as "corrupt practices" aiming to hide the original otherness by causing it to conform to a strictly target-oriented and conservative structure (1999).

The umbrella term "corruption" embraces a variety of translational behaviours defined by Danan (1991) as "nationalisation", for example the almost systematic and relatively widespread practice current in Italian audiovisual translation of aggressively appropriating the source text by converting foreign popular names into their target text equivalents, even though the addressees are perfectly capable of understanding them. In addition, working on "templates" is an ever-growing trend in the subtitling industry: templates are Rich Text files exported from subtitling software programmes and used to "maxims

DOI: 10.1057/9781137470379.0008

resources and costs" (Díaz-Cintas 2008:97). This approach, relying on a single timed subtitle file to be used by different freelancers working on the same multilingual project, proves highly effective, especially in view of the current economic crisis: in fact, "once the in and out times have been decided [...] the subtitlers are only in charge of the linguistic transfer into their native languages" (ibid.:97). Needless to say, this modus operandi, which is meant to cut the costs (software dongles, and multiple timed versions for multilingual purposes, for example), is also a way of retaining the obsolete norms set during the age of the Hollywood studio system (Nornes 1999; Díaz-Cintas in Anon. 2012). In fact, the very fact that they are precluded from performing the cueing process can only further reduce the already limited amount of freedom open to the translators themselves. Díaz-Cintas argued that:

> When the timing has been done by a professional other than the translator, the latter's freedom can be severely restricted. [...] if translators could do their own spotting, they could be more flexible and make a more rational use of the spaces needed for any given subtitle.
>
> (2005:2–3)

According to Kapsasis, the current subtitling trend in which the work is performed directly on template files is inadvisable:

> Until the early days of DVD subtitling, the subtitling process consisted in two major tasks: a technical task, [...] the timing of the subtitles, [...] and the translation, directly from the audiovisual material. Often the same person would carry out both tasks, thus fully "originating" a subtitling file.
>
> (2011:2)

Similarly, Georgakopoulou (2006:30) highlighted the fact that "thanks to the development of dedicated subtitling software, subtitlers could [...] spot the film themselves and then write their translations so as to fit the time slots they had spotted". Conversely, fansubbers, working outside the professional subtitling industry, and fulfilling the role of both "synchers" and translators, are responsible for, and are in greater control of the whole subtitling process.

As a result, in this book, the limits of mainstream practices are explored in order to encourage a debate on new approaches more in tune with the demands of the contemporary target audience and specifically addressing the issue of compartmentalisation of subtitling audiences.

DOI: 10.1057/9781137470379.0008

In his study on fansubbing, Pérez-González affirms that:

> Fansubs are subtitled versions [...] that fans (amateur subtitlers) produce primarily to express their disagreement with commercial subtitling practices and to impose linguistic and cultural mediation strategies of their own.
>
> (2007:4)

The fans' complaint concerns the process of dissimulation of the source text, and as a result, its distorted representation, since "subtitles [are] rarely used to enhance viewer awareness [...]. The defamiliarizing effect of subtitles is thus played down, since they no longer bring about a rupture of the filmic flow" (Kapsaskis 2008:8).

Against this background, a "hybrid proposal" was felt to be appropriate, namely a well-balanced blend of the best resources used both by professionals and amateur experts. In this regard, Chesterman's concept of "expectancy norms" (1997) appears to be central to this approach, as it originates precisely from what viewers expect and above all demand: "Expectancy norms are established by the expectations of readers of a translation (of a given type) concerning what a translation (of this type) should be like" (ibid.:64). Provided that the use of this theoretical framework is accepted, "source-orientedness" will be the core approach of this proposal, a method inspired by the work of Schleiermacher (1813) and further developed by Lewis (1985), Nornes (1999) and Venuti (2008). Whether we define this method as "foreignisation", "abusive fidelity" or "source-orientedness", the idea is to move from a fluent, domesticated, transparent translation to an "overt" kind of translation (House 1981), in order to preserve the cultural and linguistic flavour of the original. The successful outcome is "a translation that values experimentation, tampers with usage, seeks to match the polyvalencies [...] of the original by producing its own" (Lewis 1985:41). Hence, not only is this approach openly "source-oriented", but also "viewer-centric", since the end-viewers, with their growing demands for a revolution in the niche area of the subtitling of TV shows, are central to the reshaping of subtitling norms. Thus, having outlined the theoretical approach to translation it is now appropriate to return to the concept of expectancy norms for which translation standards are set by the expectations of the receivers. Among the main complaints made by the adherents of fansubbing is the style employed by professional subtitling, described as flattening and inconveniently imprecise.

DOI: 10.1057/9781137470379.0008

Other characteristics include the incompetent rendering of special jargon (nerdy slang, for example), cultural references (tributes to cult movies and TV shows) and inside jokes, only accessible to true connoisseurs of a specific TV series. Ultimately, this translates into a set of minor modifications to the traditional subtitling apparatus, as outlined next.

1   General aim
    To allow viewers to appreciate the audiovisual product by strictly adhering to the style, the flavour and the cultural and linguistic diversity of the original dialogues, paying particular attention to the niche audience addressed.

2   Layout
    Normally positioned on the lower part of the screen (on the upper part when on-screen text appears), subtitles should be displayed on two lines with a maximum of 45 characters per line (between 42–43 being the best option). The font colour should usually be white, but it could also be of a different colour if necessary.

3   Omission
    Translators are requested to transfer everything they can within the spatio-temporal constraints imposed. Repetitions, false starts and redundant elements should be left out, while cultural references and semantic voids should always be rendered by employing loanwords (cultural-bound expressions explicitated by notes, for example), neologisms (derived from youth culture slang) in order for obscure foreign concepts to enter the target culture.

As for duration, punctuation and segmentation, the codes of practice are exactly the same as those described in Karamitroglou and Ivarsson and Carroll's guidelines. In conclusion, this proposal stems from specific theoretical approaches giving prominence to faithfulness in translation in order to come to a set of norms allowing increased freedom to subtitlers. Thus, subtitles would no longer act as guidance, but as a vehicle able to convey cultural and linguistic "otherness" where the touch of the subtitler is made visible. In the next chapter, which is focused on the case study of the American TV show *Lost*, the consequences of the resistance of amateurs will be examined in depth, showing how subtitling professionals seem to have taken advantage of fansubbed versions without acknowledging their contribution.

DOI: 10.1057/9781137470379.0008

Notes

1   Available at: www.esist.org/ESIST%20Subtitling%20code_files/Code%20of%20 Good%20Subtitling%20Practice_en.pdf.

2   Note that it is common practice to follow the six-second rule (D'Ydewalle et al. 1987; Brondeel 1994).

3   For example: NORMAL or 264, HD or 720p, FULL HD or 1080p, WEB-DL from iTunes, and DVDRip from DVDs, depending on the resolution chosen for the video.

4   In order to explain their work, ItaSA uploaded two interesting videos on www.youtube.com:

    Itasa Faq 1.1: www.youtube.com/
      watch?feature=player_embedded&v=IxsoogaEvek#!.
    Itasa Faq 1.2: www.youtube.com/
      watch?feature=player_embedded&v=4crg1L3pI9g.

5   My translation. In the original: "La guida che andrete a leggere è il risultato di anni di traduzioni, di discussioni tra subber e revisori. Serve come vademecum fin dalla vostra prima traduzione e contiene le principali regole di grammatica italiana. La lettura della presente guida non è facoltativa, è obbligatoria per tutti e la traduzione deve avvenire secondo le convenzioni indicate".

DOI: 10.1057/9781137470379.0008

5
Origin of the Italian Fansubbing Phenomenon

Abstract: *The following section is devoted to the analysis of a case study focusing on the TV show* Lost. *It is the first part of a comparative analysis of episode 1 of the second season and episode 1 of the final season of the show (described in Chapter 6), aiming to identify the key features characteristic of fansubbing and trace the evolution of the methodologies used by amateurs over time. As far as translation, line length and characters per second, text on screen and position of subtitles, measurements and conversion, timing and workflow are concerned, the progress made by fansubbers is traced by comparing the fansubbed and subtitled versions, in order to measure the quality of their work over a six-year period.*

Massidda, Serenella. *Audiovisual Translation in the Digital Age: The Italian Fansubbing Phenomenon.* Basingstoke: Palgrave Macmillan, 2015.
DOI: 10.1057/9781137470379.0009.

The following section is devoted to the analysis of a case study focusing on the TV show *Lost*.

It is a comparative analysis of episode 1 of the second season and episode 1 of the final season of *Lost*, aiming to identify the key features of fansubbing and trace the evolution of amateurs' methodologies over time. The progress made by fansubbers as far as translation, line length and characters per second, text on screen and position of subtitles, measurements and conversion, timing and workflow are concerned, is traced by comparing the fansubbed and the subtitled versions, in order to measure the quality of their work over a six-year period.

5.1   *Lost*: from initial struggle to happy ending

Lost is a sci-fi TV show created by J. Lieber, J. J. Abrams and D. Lindelof and aired on ABC from September 2004 to May 2010. It is an account of the 324 survivors of Oceanic Airlines Flight 815 which crashed on a deserted tropical island. For the first time on TV, the audience was presented with a complex, nonlinear storyline developed with an extensive use of "flash-sideways", a combination of flash-backs and flash-forwards, served with a pinch of mythological elements and written using a multiple narrative perspective device called "polyphonic narrative" (Cate 2009).

With such narrative novelties, along with the large ensemble cast and the cost of filming, mostly set in the breathtaking location of Oahu, Hawaii, it is no small wonder that it was to become the most success-ful TV drama of all time. As a way to trace the evolution of fansubbing practices, in the case study under analysis, episode 1 of the second season of *Lost*, broadcast in Italy in 2005, is investigated and compared with the first episode of the final season. It was decided to start with the second season rather than the first owing to the issue of workflow standardisa-tion. In fact, while during the first season the communities' approach to fansubbing was relatively casual and erratic, they began to employ a set of translation guidelines and a series of cueing standards that permitted a reliable analysis of the process from season 2 on.

5.1.1   Key features of fansubbing

The following investigation takes into account three different versions of "Man of Science, Man of Faith" (*Lost*, season 2, episode 1): ItaSA's,

Subsfactory's and the official version commercialised on DVD. The main traits of fansubbing will be highlighted through the use of screenshots and the various mistranslations, formatting and cueing mistakes made by the two fan groups during the very first stage of their work as translators will be examined, comparing them with professional standards. We will analyse a set of features common to fansubbing attempting to distinguish among different translation issues, namely line length and characters per second, text on screen, measurements and conversions, terminology and mistranslations and interference from other audio-visual translations modes.

5.1.2   Line length and characters per second

The first topic under analysis is line length of the subtitles, shown in Table 5.1, which displays the DVD and the fansubbed versions (*Lost*, season 2, episode 1).

TABLE 5.1   Lost – *season 2, episode 1*

Original Dialogue – *Lost* season 2, episode 1	
and blow open the hatch, and then you're gonna hide everyone inside.	
DVD Version	**Fansubbed Version (Subsfactory)**
00:00:10,670 –> 00:00:13,955 far esplodere una botola e far nascondere tutti lì dentro.	00:00:10,670 –> 00:00:13,955 e far saltare il portello, e poi fare nascondere tutti dentro. **(62 characters on a one-liner)**

The standard characters allowed in mainstream subtitling (37–40 characters) and fansubbing (45 characters) have been listed in Chapter 4 where we have compared subtitling and fansubbing standards. Even though fansubbing guidelines allow for 45 characters per line, Table 5.1 shows an editing mistake on the part of subbers, a one-liner composed of 62 characters that literally invade the bottom of the screen thus making it inconveniently long and hard for the viewers to read. On the other hand, the table also shows how the same subtitle is rendered with a two-liner and a good formatting procedure in the DVD version.

A parallel topic is the one relating to cps (characters per second) constraint. It is extremely important to strike a balance between the number of characters employed and the time exposure of the subtitle.

DOI: 10.1057/9781137470379.0009

Once again, Subtitle Workshop developers created an add-in programme called CPS Auto-checker in order to verify that the harmony between the parameters noted above is always achieved. In the following example showing an extract from season 2, episode 1 of *Lost* (Table 5.2), fansubbers produced a two-liner made up of a total of 95 characters within a time span of nearly three seconds which is highlighted in red (see screenshot 5.1, bottom left) as a mistake by the CPS Auto-checker.

TABLE 5.2   Lost – *season 2, episode 1*

Original Dialogue – *Lost* season 2, episode 1	
We left to blow it open so that we could hide inside.	
DVD Version	**Fansubbed Version (Subsfactory)**
00:04:46,065 –> 00:04:49,062 Abbiamo aperto la botola Per poterci mettere al sicuro.	00:04:46,065 –> 00:04:49,062 abbiamo fatto saltare il portello così possiamo mettere ognuno lì dentro... saranno al sicuro... **(47/48 characters)**

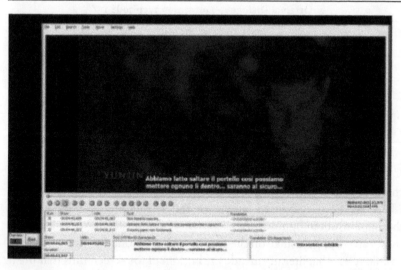

FIGURE 5.1   *Screenshot – CPS Auto-checker*

In the official version above, we can see that the source text is condensed and that the characters per second limitation is balanced with the time exposure of the subtitle, while some redundant elements were thus sacrificed.

DOI: 10.1057/9781137470379.0009

5.1.3   Text on screen and position of subtitles

In the following example taken from season 2, episode 1 of *Lost* (screenshots 5.2 A–B), the issue of non-verbal visual signs and text on screen is addressed. The images show a keyboard key sign and its translation into Italian.

In Subsfactory's version the visual sign comes untranslated. In fact, in the early stages of fansubbing, this type of mistake was quite frequent, so

FIGURE 5.2A   *Screenshot – DVD*

FIGURE 5.2B   *Screenshot – Subsfactory*

DOI: 10.1057/9781137470379.0009

that it appears that either the subbers did not consider it appropriate to translate it or perhaps it simply passed unnoticed. Conversely, fansubbers sometimes added subtitles even if it was unnecessary, for example in the following image (screenshot 5.3) taken from season 2, episode 1 of *Lost*, where a character utters "shush!" the equivalent fansub reads "Shh.".

FIGURE 5.3   *Screenshot – Subsfactory*

As a rule, interjections are always omitted in professional subtitling because the viewers immediately recognise the communicative intention behind them. Words like "oh" and "ehm" and so on do not need any translation as they are universally understood and also because the image speaks for itself. Yet, they are transcribed by fansubbers as if they were producing SDH subtitles. This tendency may be due to the source text employed, the so-called "ts", a sort of transcription of TV captions (see Chapter 3 for more details).

Following on from the issue of text on screen, let us turn to the issue of on-screen text. Both ItaSA and Subsfactory's fansubbed versions, at this stage, would always display the subtitles over the text on screen, making them confusing and sloppy, while obscuring the initial credits of the show. It might have been that, at that time, fansubbers were not yet able to master the use of the subtitling software employed. In Subtitle Workshop, one of the most frequently used open source software programs, the position of the subtitles is controlled by various tags (for example {\an8} to raise the subtitle on top), hence by just adding {\an8} at the beginning of the subtitle, it simply moves upwards. However, later on in the episode, we find that fansubbers from both ItaSA and Subsfactory

DOI: 10.1057/9781137470379.0009

raised only a single subtitle to the top of the screen so as not to overwrite the text on screen. Thus, at this stage, this practice was sometimes used in fansubbing, but it probably depended on the tastes of the revisor and/ or on the popularity of the TV show translated.

A frequent mistake encountered in the fansubbed versions is the translation of the subject pronoun into Italian. As a rule, subject pronouns are regularly omitted in Italian, since the verb form indicates the subject. Table 5.3 shows how the DVD version omits the subject pronoun in favour of a more fluent and less literal translation.

TABLE 5.3   Lost – *season 2, episode 1*

Original Dialogue – *Lost* season 2, episode 1	
We'll never get everyone down in time.	
DVD Version	**Subsfactory's Version**
00:04:50,909 –> 00:04:52,667 Non riusciremo mai a far scendere tutti in tempo.	00:04:50,909 –> 00:04:52,667 **Noi** non metteremo tutti lì dentro in tempo.

In addition, the fact that fewer characters have been used allows for a better adaptation.

5.1.4   Measurements and conversion

During the translation phase, the professional subtitling practice is to convert measurements as a way of facilitating the comprehension of the target audience. In Table 5.4 we show how Subsfactory's version leaves

TABLE 5.4   Lost – *season 2, episode 1*

Original Dialogue – *Lost* season 2, episode 1	
Kate: – 40 **feet** down John: – 50, tops	
ItaSA's Version	**Subsfactory's Version**
▸ Circa 12 **metri** dal fondo? ▸ Al massimo 15.	▸ 40 **piedi** di profondità? ▸ 50.
DVD Version	
▸ Saranno 12 **metri**? ▸ 15 al Massimo.	

DOI: 10.1057/9781137470379.0009

the original imperial measurement (feet) without converting it into its metric equivalent, while in ItaSA's fansubs and in the DVD version the measurement has been converted.

Once again, in this stage, the behaviour of the fansubbers has proved to be erratic. As shown in Table 5.4, in the source dialogue the characters say: "Kate: – 40 feet down/John: – 50, tops": ItaSA's conversion, in fact, is correct and the translation is almost the same as the official one.

5.1.5   Interferences from dubbese

Every once in a while, other audiovisual translation "modes" may interfere with amateur translation practices. Influences from "dubbese", (cf. Antonini 2008; Bucaria 2008; Chaume 2004b; Cipolloni 1996; D'Aversa 1996; Filmer 2011; Galassi 1996; Herbst 1987, Pavesi 2005, 2008; Raffaelli 1994; Rossi 1999, 2002), as opposed to ordinary speech, a variety of the language of dubbing characterised by unrealistic features, are prevalent in fansubbing versions.

> The term dubbese (in Italian "doppiaggese") was coined by Italian screen translators and operators to negatively connote the linguistic hybrid that over the years has emerged as the standard variety of Italian spoken by characters in dubbed filmic products both for TV and cinema. Indeed, the use of dubbese for the transposition into Italian of both fictional and non-fictional filmic products has become so widespread that Italian screen operators themselves [...] started expressing the concern that it might leak out and affect authentic, every day spoken Italian, particularly that of children.
>
> (Antonini 2008:136)

Apparently, the prefabricated, artificial spoken language adopted in dubbed films resorts to calques from American English, along with anglicisms, in order to create a touch of orality. Although the neologisms created by dubbese do not belong to the Italian spoken language, they have, nevertheless, become part of conversational routines in film dialogues (Filmer 2011). Table 5.5 is an example of the hybridisation between this variety of language and the amateur subtitling style.

The source text reads: "The French woman is missing a bloody wing nut". While in the DVD version the translation tends to mitigate the effects of the original expression (back translation: "the French woman has a screw loose"), in Subsfactory's it is rendered quite literally, using the expression "fottuta pazza" (back translation: "fucking crazy"), where the

TABLE 5.5   Lost – *season 2, episode 1*

Original Dialogue – *Lost* season 2, episode 1	
The French woman is missing a bloody wing nut.	
DVD Version	**Back Translation**
Alla francese <u>manca una rotella</u>.	The French woman has a **screw loose**.
Subsfactory's Version	**Back Translation**
La donna francese è una <u>fottuta pazza</u>, sapete?	The French woman is **fucking crazy**, you know?

Italian adjective "fottuta" is a loan from dubbese, the "hybrid language used by the Italian dubbing industry to transpose both fictional and non-fictional foreign TV and cinema productions" (Antonini and Chiaro 2009:3). Dubbing routines, in fact, have a tendency to employ the adjectival intensifier "fottuta" in order to render the American English equivalent of "fucking", "frigging" and "bloody", for example. Fansubbers seem to act similarly when dealing with these aspects of language, perhaps because they have been exposed to dubbing for too long a period.

It is surely worth noting that the translation of the term "dude" constitutes another interesting case in the TV show (Table 5.6).

At times, translating apparently superfluous words (for example vocatives) serves the valuable purpose of conveying the source text style. The

TABLE 5.6   Lost – *season 2, episode 1*

Original Dialogue – *Lost* season 2, episode 1	
I really don't want to, dude. I love those commercials.	
DVD Version	**Back Translation**
▸ Non mi va. ▸ Adoro quella pubblicità.	▸ I don't want to. ▸ I love those commercials.
Subsfactory's Version	**Back Translation**
Davvero, non mi va, <u>bello</u>.	Really, I don't want to, **handsome**.
ItaSA's Version	**Back Translation**
Preferirei non farlo, <u>coso</u>.	I'd rather not to, **thing**.

DOI: 10.1057/9781137470379.0009

example shown in Table 5.6 attempts to shed light on style, an aspect often neglected by mainstream subtitling, in fact, this colloquial method of addressing a person is systematically omitted. As a result, the translation of the vocative term in question is rather important if we are to analyse the protagonist of the scene, Hugo "Hurley" Reyes, played by Jorge Garcia, *Lost*'s comic relief. The term "dude", a clearly redundant vocative form, turns out to be a perfect vehicle able to convey the actor's characterisation of Hurley. As shown in the table, in the DVD version, "dude" has no equivalent and simply disappeared. In their fansubbed version, ItaSA, quite creatively, has opted for the neologism "coso" (back translation: "thing" plus the male suffix -o), a choice heavily influenced by dubbing. On the other hand, Subsfactory translated the vocative "dude" with "bello" (back translation: "handsome"), which is also a creative use of the word taken from dubbese, although almost non-existent in the Italian spoken language. As a rule, professional subtitling guidelines omit redundant elements considered to be irrelevant, and apparently, there is no need to convey such nuances of language, yet it is sometimes essential to include them in order to reproduce the style of the original version. The omission of these vocative forms is interpreted by fansubbers as a failing, hence their tendency to translate everything. The translation of "everything" belonging to the original dialogue, one of the peculiarities of fansubbing, is due to the rigid principle of remaining as faithful as possible to the foreign audiovisual product. However, the reason behind this obsessive preoccupation could also be due to the specific cueing standards of fansubbing. Amateur experts believe that subtitles should start with the first sound uttered by a character, and, even if the sound does not constitute a proper word, they believe that it should be rendered anyhow. This is how fansubbers perceive the timing process and, consequently, how they originate and produce the subtitles.

5.1.6   Mistranslations

At an earlier stage of fansubbing, a distinguishing trait was that of source text mistranslations. In the scene under analysis, shown in Table 5.7, we have a flashback set in the E.R. where one of the characters (Jack) used to work before the plane crashed on the mysterous island.

A patient arrives and the nurse introduces her case saying: "Female, late twenties, no ID". Subsfactory translated it as follows: "Femmina in ritardo 20s, nessuna identificazione", where "late" refers to the woman

TABLE 5.7   Lost – *season 2, episode 1*

Original Dialogue – *Lost* season 2, episode 1	
Female, late twenties, no ID.	
Subsfactory's Version	**Back Translation**
Femmina in ritardo 20s, nessuna identificazione.	Female, **late, 20s**, no ID.
ItaSA's Version	**Back Translation**
Femmina, sui 20 anni, nessuna identificazione.	Female, **around 20 years old**, no ID.
DVD Version	**Back Translation**
Femmina, vent'anni.	Female, **20 years old**.

who "seems to be late", producing a sentence that does not make sense at all. ItaSA's version, instead, reads as follows: "Femmina, sui 20 anni, nessuna identificazione" (back translation: "Female, around 20 years old, no ID). On the other hand, the DVD version leaves out the fact that she has no ID and produces a two liner adding another piece of information: "She coded twice".

Another interesting case of mistranslation on the part of fansubbers is shown in Table 5.8.

TABLE 5.8   Lost – *season 2, episode 1*

Original Dialogue – *Lost* season 2, episode 1	
I was buying a frozen burrito and thought "I should play the lottery".	
Subsfactory's Version	**Back Translation**
Stavo comprando un gelato, ed pensai, "ehi, dovrei giocare alla/ lotteria."	I was buying an **icecream** and thought, "ehi, I should play/the **lottery**".
ItaSA's Version	**Back Translation**
Stavo comprando un burrito fritto, e ho pensato, "ehi, potrei giocare alla lotteria".	I was buying a **deep fried burrito** and thought, "ehi, I could play the **lottery**".
DVD Version	**Back Translation**
Stavo comprando un burrito quando ho pensato di giocare al lotto.	I was buying a **burrito** When I thought to play the **lotto**.

DOI: 10.1057/9781137470379.0009

In the professional version the word "lottery" is adapted and rendered as "lotto", for no apparent reason, since "lotteria" is the perfect equivalent in the target language. The translation in the DVD version is quite arbitrary, but is still acceptable. In Subsfactory's fansubs, "burrito" becomes "ice cream" ("gelato"), while in ItaSA's translation "frozen" becomes "deep fried" ("fritto"). This kind of mistakes may unintentionally appear to be quite hilarious, yet it reveals the level of inaccuracy of the two fansubbing communities at this particular stage in their work.

Another example (Table 5.9) concerns the source text expression "chicken joint" which was rendered as follows:

TABLE 5.9   Lost – *season 2, episode 1*

Original Dialogue – *Lost* season 2, episode 1	
The chicken joint where I worked at got hit by a meteor.	
Subsfactory's Version	**Back Translation**
La chicken joint dove lavoravo fu colpita da una meteora...	The **chicken joint** where I worked was hit by a **meteor**.
ItaSA's Version	**Back Translation**
La catena di polli per cui lavoravo è stata colpita da una stella cadente.	The **chain of chickens** where I worked was hit by a **shooting star**.
DVD Version	**Back Translation**
E il fast food dove lavoravo è stato colpito da una meteora...	And the **fast food reastaurant** where I worked was hit by a **meteor**.

While the DVD version translates it correctly as "fast food", by employing a hypernym which defines a specific kind of restaurants, Subsfactory leaves it untranslated and ItaSA makes up a neologism, "catena di polli" (back translation: chain of chickens) which has no meaning in the target language. As a matter of fact, the character in question (Harley) used to work at "Mr. Clucks", a chicken restaurant, or more precisely a fast food joint specialised in chicken. In the case of Subsfactory, at a very early stage of fansubbing, a sort of "loanword strategy" was used every time the transfer of certain concepts was unclear. On the other hand, ItaSA employed a calque where an Italian equivalent was ready-made: the hypernym "fast food" is sufficient to explain the source text expression even if it does not specify the type of food served in this kind of restaurant.

DOI: 10.1057/9781137470379.0009

The following example focuses on the translation of the term "folks", which in American English is used to address a group of people in an informal way. This is illustrated in Table 5.10:

TABLE 5.10   Lost – *season 2, episode 1*

Original Dialogue – *Lost* season 2, episode 1	
Wait for the brave folks on the raft to bring help.	
Subsfactory's Version	**Back Translation**
Aspettiamo i <u>popoli coraggiosi</u> sulla zattera che ci portano aiuto.	Let's wait for **the brave peoples** on the raft who bring help.
ItaSA's Version	**Back Translation**
Aspettare i "<u>nostri eroi</u>" sulla zattera che ci portino gli aiuti.	Wait for **our heroes** on the raft who bring help.
DVD Version	**Back Translation**
Aspettare che <u>quelli della zattera</u> chiedano aiuto.	Wait that **those of the raft** ask for help.

In this scene, one of the characters suggests that the party should wait for a group of survivors who tried to get away from the island in order to ask for help because the "others", or the enemies, were coming. Table 5.10 shows how the source text expression "brave folks" was rendered in the three versions: the official translation opted for levelling out the source text and omitted the adjective "brave", while ItaSA's choice was to employ the strategy of explicitation by transposing the concept elicited by the term "brave" into the noun "eroi" ("heroes"). Subsfactory, unfortunately, gave a literal rendering of the expression, consequently misrepresenting the intended meaning of "folks" with "peoples" ("popoli"). Professional subtitlers, occasionally, can make ghastly mistakes, and the following example (Table 5.11) shows a significant case of mistranslation. The scene in the E.R. mentioned in Table 5.7 continues and another patient is brought in by the paramedics.

The table shows the three different versions examined and particularly how the source text term "collar" was rendered: the problem revolves around the polysemy of the term "collar" that may refer to a body part, a garment or a medical device. Its meaning is, in fact, apparently quite clear: a wounded patient has just entered the emergency room and is wearing a collar in order to keep his neck straight and to support the

DOI: 10.1057/9781137470379.0009

TABLE 5.11   *Lost – season 2, episode 1*

Original Dialogue – *Lost* season 2, episode 1	
A piece of the steering column. Let's go. Keep that collar steady.	
Subsfactory's Version	**Back Translation**
Ok iniziamo... tieni quel <u>colletto</u> fermo.	Ok, let's start. Keep the **collar of the shirt** steady.
ItaSA's Version	**Back Translation**
Va bene, cominciamo. Bloccate il <u>collare</u>.	Ok, let's start. Keep the **cervical collar** steady.
DVD Version	**Back Translation**
Un pezzo dello sterzo. Avanti. Tenete ferma la <u>clavicola</u>.	A piece of the steering column. Let's go. Keep that **collar-bone** steady.

head. Hence, just by translating what is represented in the images, it is certainly evident that the correct translation is the one produced by ItaSA which selected the correct equivalent translating it as "cervical collar". In this case, the DVD version shows a total misinterpretation of the source dialogue: owing to the fact that the action is well-explained by the images, it seems like the scene in question was translated without accessing the associated video.

Another case of mistranslation on the part of professionals, and related to medical terminology, is illustrated in Table 5.12.

In the scene analysed, the doctor introduced in the previous example is talking to a patient about her medical diagnosis. The source text expression, "fracture dislocation" is rendered as "frattura dislocata" in the DVD version, while the correct Italian medical terminology should be "frattura scomposta", and the term "spine", rendered as "spina", ought to be "rachide" in the target language. This kind of mistake demonstrates the poor quality of terminology research on the part of professional subtitlers in contrast to ItaSA's more accurate translation of the same medical expressions, where "spine" is rendered as "spina dorsale" which is a perfectly acceptable variation of "rachide".

The last instance of mistranslation on the part of subtitlers revolves around the meaning of the verb "roll around" (Table 5.13). In one of the many flashbacks in the TV show, the main character's flow of thought

TABLE 5.12   Lost – *season 2, episode 1*

Original Dialogue – *Lost* season 2, episode 1	
You have a fracture dislocation of your thoracic lumbar spine.	
DVD Version	**Back Translation**
Ha una _frattura dislocata_ della spina lombare.	You have a **dislocated fracture** of the lumbar spine.
ItaSA's Version	**Back Translation**
Ha una _frattura scomposta_ della _spina dorsale toracica e lombare._	You have a **fracture dislocation** of the **thoracic and lumbar spine**.

TABLE 5.13   Lost – *season 2, episode 1*

Original Dialogue – *Lost* season 2, episode 1	
I can still roll around at my wedding.	
DVD Version	**Back Translation**
Ma posso sempre _rotolare_ al mio matrimonio.	I can always **roll** at my wedding.
ItaSA's Version	**Back Translation**
Ma potrò ancora _comportarmi normalmente_ al mio matrimonio.	But I can still **behave normally** at my wedding.

sends the viewer back to a time when, before the air crash, he used to work as a doctor and was talking to one of his patients. In the scene, the woman in question was about to get married when she had an accident in which she was left completely paralysed.

The phrasal verb "to roll round" defines the activity of moving on wheels, or using a wheelchair. In the DVD version it was translated simply as "roll" ("rotolare"), which seems rather misinterpreted and totally out of context. ItaSA, on the other hand, came up with a free translation into Italian, "comportarmi normalmente" (back translation: "behave normally"), which bears no relation to the source language verb.

DOI: 10.1057/9781137470379.0009

6

Evolution of ItaSA
and Subsfactory

Abstract: *This chapter focuses on the case study of the US TV show* Lost *(part 2), the consequences of the resistance to dubbing and mainstream subtitling on the part of amateurs is examined in depth, showing how subtitling professionals appear to take advantage of fansubbed versions without acknowledging their contribution. The changes made by the two communities over time are analysed (*Lost, *season 6, episode 1) in this section and the features which have remained unaffected are also examined. The benefits and drawbacks of faithfulness in translation, text compression and omission, condensation, style, register and typographical conventions are among the topics covered.*

Massidda, Serenella. *Audiovisual Translation in the Digital Age: The Italian Fansubbing Phenomenon.* Basingstoke: Palgrave Macmillan, 2015. DOI: 10.1057/9781137470379.0010.

In this chapter, which, as we have noted, focuses on the case study of the US TV show *Lost* (part 2), the consequences of the resistance to dubbing and mainstream subtitling on the part of amateurs is examined in depth, showing how subtitling professionals appear to take advantage of fansubbed versions without acknowledging their contribution.

The sixth and final season of *Lost* was aired in Italy in 2010, almost in real time with the United States. What is more, on 24 May 2010, a unique event took place: the final episode of the series was aired simultaneously by NBC in the United States, Sky1 in the United Kingdom, Fox Italia in Italy and many more countries worldwide. In Italy, the episode was aired in English at 6.00 'am, and fansubbed by ItaSA and Subsfactory a few hours later. It was then re-aired 24 hours later with Italian "pro-subtitles" and eventually broadcast on 31 May 2010 in its dubbed Italian version.

Never before had Italians experienced such a speed in dealing with audiovisual translation. It is no small wonder that the Italian fansubbing movement paved the way for this to happen. Five years later, after the first steps into audiovisual translation had been taken by the fansubbing communities, we are able to attest to a significant number of developments in various areas of the phenomenon.

Firstly, fansubbers do not simply translate, as they used to at the beginning, but they also originate the subtitles, a role carried out solely by the so-called "synchers". Nowadays, this practice has been adopted by both communities, meaning that there are more specialised fansubbers and a brand new assembly line.

The advantages and disadvantages of faithfulness in translation, text compression and omission, condensation, style and typographical conventions are among the topics covered. The changes made by ItaSA and Subsfactory are analysed in this section (*Lost*, season 6, episode 1) and the features which have remained unaffected are also examined.

6.1   Faithfulness in translation: pros and cons

Episode 1 of the final season of *Lost*, "La X", starts with the beautiful image of a galleon sailing on the ocean (screenshots 6.1 A–C):
The character uttering the words in the subtitles is complaining about the enemies, also known as "the others" (see Table 6.1).

In this case, the versions produced by ItaSA and Subsfactory are almost identical. The verb "corrupt" is rendered rather literally by the

DOI: 10.1057/9781137470379.0010

Italian "corrompono" (back translation: "corrupt/bribe"), although there is a problem in that it acts as a transitive verb, meaning that it must be followed by a direct object or the resulting sentence would be grammatically incomplete. A good equivalent is found in the DVD version where the subtitler has opted for "rovinano tutto" (back translation, "they ruin everything"), which conveys the exact meaning of the source text.

FIGURE 6.1A   *Screenshot (ENG) – DVD*

FIGURE 6.1B   *Screenshot (IT) – DVD*

DOI: 10.1057/9781137470379.0010

FIGURE 6.1C   *Screenshot – Subsfactory*

TABLE 6.1   Lost – *season 6, episode 1*

Original Dialogue – *Lost* season 6, episode 1	
they corrupt. It always ends the same.	
DVD Version	**Back Translation**
e <u>rovinano tutto</u>. Finisce sempre così.	And they **ruin everything**. It always ends the same.
ItaSA's Version	**Back Translation**
<u>Corrompono</u>. Finisce sempre allo stesso modo.	They **corrupt/bribe**. It ends always at the same way.
Subsfactory's Version	**Back Translation**
<u>Corrompono</u>. Finisce sempre allo stesso modo.	They **corrupt/bribe**. It ends always at the same way.

After all these seasons, what seems to remain unchanged in the behaviour of the fansubbers is the tendency to remain scrupulously faithful to the source text, even if it is sometimes absolutely unnecessary. Fansubbers apparently strive towards a slavish adherence to their own guidelines and believe that faithfulness to the original dialogue should be paramount, a dominant trait which could result in undermining their ability to adapt the original dialogues to suit the target language and to produce a more

DOI: 10.1057/9781137470379.0010

fluent translation. This trait becomes apparent in the following scene, where no mistake is actually made. However, the example in question gives us a hint of their attitude towards translation (Table 6.2).

"Detonate" is translated as "detonare" in both fansubbed versions (Table 6.2), while in the official translation it is rendered as "esplodere" that shows a different etymological root from the English term.

The tendency to extreme faithfulness can also be found in the next example (shown in Table 6.3), where the translation in the fansubbed

TABLE 6.2   Lost – *season 6, episode 1*

Original Dialogue – *Lost* season 6, episode 1	
I think I can negate that energy. I'm gonna detonate a hydrogen bomb.	
DVD Version	**Back Translation**
Posso annullare l'energia. Farò <u>esplodere</u> una bomba all'idrogeno.	I can negate the energy. I will **explode** a hydrogen bomb.
ITASA'S Version	**Back Translation**
Credo di poter annullare quell'energia. Farò <u>detonare</u> una bomba a idrogeno.	I think I can negate that energy. I will **detonate** a hydrogen bomb.
Subsfactory's Version	**Back Translation**
Penso di poter annullare quell'energia. Farò <u>detonare</u> una bomba all'idrogeno.	I think I can negate that energy. I will **detonate** a hydrogen bomb.

TABLE 6.3   Lost – *season 6, episode 1*

Original Dialogue – *Lost* season 6, episode 1	
I have tortured more people than I can remember.	
DVD Version	**Back Translation**
Non ricordo neanche quante persone ho torturato.	I even can't remember how many people I have tortured.
ItaSA's Version	**Back Translation**
Ho torturato più persone di quante ne riesca a ricordare.	I have tortured more people than I can remember.
Subsfactory's Version	**Back Translation**
Ho torturato più persone di quante riesca a ricordare.	I have tortured more people than I can remember.

DOI: 10.1057/9781137470379.0010

version results in a literal rendering, producing an awkwardly incoherent translation, while a better solution is offered by the official translation.

The back translation of the source dialogue in the DVD version reads, "I even can't remember how many people I have tortured", while Subsfactory and ItaSA's Italian syntactic structures are almost identical to those of the source language, producing an influent and twisted equivalent in the target text.

The following example (Table 6.4) focuses on the option to translate or omit the word "man" found in the source text sentence: "you shouldn't let that happen, man".

TABLE 6.4 Lost – *season 6, episode 1*

Original Dialogue – *Lost* season 6, episode 1	
You should've let that happen, <u>man.</u>	
DVD Version	**Back Translation**
Non saresti dovuto intervenire.	You shouldn't have intervened.
ItaSA's Version	**Back Translation**
Avresti dovuto lasciare che accadesse, <u>bello</u>.	You should've let that happen, **handsome**.
Subsfactory's Version	**Back Translation**
Avresti dovuto lasciare che succedesse, <u>amico</u>.	You should've let that happen, **friend**.

In mainstream subtitling, this colloquial method of addressing a person is systematically omitted, although fansubbers believe that it is important to translate these seemingly superfluous words (cf. Table 5.6). There is, apparently, no need to convey nuances of language, yet it is sometimes essential to include them in order to characterise both the style and register of the original version, as we have demonstrated in Table 5.6 with the translation of the word "dude". The character uttering this sentence speaks in an English accent, and he is also a drug addict who has just attempted to swallow a huge quantitative of heroin, as we can infer from the scene, so that the addition of a simple word like "man" might help to convey some of the peculiarities of his behaviour and background. Moreover, the omission of these apparently meaningless and redundant vocative forms (above all at the end of subtitles) is seemingly interpreted by fansubbers as a failing, hence their tendency to translate everything. As shown in Table 6.4, the DVD version omits the

DOI: 10.1057/9781137470379.0010

term "man", displaying a very aseptic subtitle, while Subsfactory translates it literally as "amico" ("friend") in a style reminiscent of dubbese and ItaSA attempts to adapt it by employing the word "bello" ("handsome"), which, although it is not used very frequently in Italian, can be found in some sub-varieties of standard language or youth slang used in specific regions of the country.

The same behaviour can be found in the rendering of the words "mate" (in the original sentence: "so mate, do you mind if I sit here?"), and "brother" (uttered with an Irish accent, hence strongly marked), respectively fansubbed using the equivalent Italian term "amico" (friend) and "fratello" (brother), and, once again, omitted in the professional version (tables 6.5 and 6.6):

The translation of everything belonging to the original dialogues, which is one of the peculiarities of fansubbing, is due to the rigid principle of remaining as faithful as possible to the foreign audiovisual product. Yet, the reason behind this obsessive preoccupation with inserting vocatives, false starts and hesitations could also be due to the specific cueing standards of fansubbing. As we have already seen in the preceding sections (cf. Chapter 4), the communities analysed believe that subtitles should start with the first sound uttered by a character, and, even if the sound does not constitute a proper word (e.g. hesitations, false starts and the like), they believe that it should be rendered anyhow. In addition, given that the script employed by subbers (the so-called "ts") is derived from the closed subtitling or captioning files

TABLE 6.5   Lost – *season 6, episode 1*

Original Dialogue – *Lost* season 6, episode 1	
Oh, I'm sorry, mate. Is this your seat?	
DVD Version	**Back Translation**
Ti spiace se sto qui?	Do you mind if I sit here?
ItaSA's Version	**Back Translation**
<u>Amico</u>, ti spiace se mi siedo qui?	**Friend**, do you mind if I sit here?
Subsfactory's Version	**Back Translation**
Senti, <u>amico</u>, è un problema se sto seduto qui?	Listen, **mate**, is it a problem if I sit here?

DOI: 10.1057/9781137470379.0010

TABLE 6.6   Lost – *season 6, episode 1*

Original Dialogue – *Lost* season 6, episode 1	
▸ Yeah, no problem	
▸ Thanks, brother.	
DVD Version	**Back Translation**
▸ Non c'è problema.	▸ No problem.
▸ Grazie mille.	▸ Thanks a lot.
ItaSA's Version	**Back Translation**
▸ Sì, nessun problema.	▸ Yes, no problem.
▸ Grazie, <u>fratello</u>.	▸ Thanks, **brother**.
Subsfactory's Version	**Back Translation**
▸ Certo, non c'è problema.	▸ Of course, no problem.
▸ Grazie, <u>fratello</u>.	▸ Thanks, **brother**.

meant for viewers with an aural or hearing impairment (SDH subtitling), the norms governing this type of transfer are completely different, as is its end purpose. An example based on the repetition of "no" is given below (Table 6.7).

TABLE 6.7   Lost – *season 6, episode 1*

Original Dialogue – *Lost* season 6, episode 1	
▸ Something wrong?	
▸ No. No, you just...	
DVD Version	**Back Translation**
▸ Qualcosa non va?	▸ Something wrong?
▸ No, è solo che...	▸ No, it's just that...
ItaSA's Version	**Back Translation**
▸ C'è qualcosa che non va?	▸ Something wrong?
▸ <u>No, no</u>, è solo che...	▸ **No, no**, it's just that...
Subsfactory's Version	**Back Translation**
▸ Qualcosa non va?	▸ Something wrong?
▸ <u>No, no</u>. È solo...	▸ **No, no**. It's just...

DOI: 10.1057/9781137470379.0010

On the other hand, professional versions can also be quite literal at times. The original dialogue belonging to the scene shown below – focusing on time travel – reads: "Blown up, just like we left it, before we started jumping through time". Here the expression "jump through time" has a perfect equivalent in Italian, "viaggiare nel tempo" (back translation: "travel through time"). Literally transposing the verb "jump" into Italian results in a translation that reads as a "translation" (see Table 6.8).

TABLE 6.8   Lost – *season 6, episode 1*

Original Dialogue – *Lost* season 6, episode 1	
Blown up, just like we left it, before we started jumping through time.	
DVD Version	**Back Translation**
Esplosa! Come l'avevamo lasciata prima che cominciassimo a <u>saltare nel tempo</u>.	Exploded! Like we had left it before we started to **jump through time**.
ItaSA's Version	**Back Translation**
Proprio come l'abbiamo lasciata prima di cominciare a <u>saltare qua e là nel tempo</u>.	Just like we left it before we started to **jump here and there through time**.
Subsfactory's Version	**Back Translation**
Proprio come l'avevamo lasciata, prima che iniziassimo a <u>viaggiare nel tempo</u>.	Just like we left it, before we started to **travel through time**.

Conversely, while ItaSA reproduces the same mistranslation, Subsfactory, quite professionally, recognises the correct equivalent and translates it into Italian as "travel".

6.2   Text compression and omission

A hybrid approach to future subtitling standards is proposed in Chapter 4, which is devoted to a comparison between subtitling and fansubbing norms. In this section, the topic of condensation in subtitling will be treated so as to clarify what is reduced in both fansubbing and subtitling translations and why. A comparison between the amateur and professional translational approaches may be useful in order to understand the strategies at work in both environments.

DOI: 10.1057/9781137470379.0010

The following (Table 6.9) is an excellent example of how mainstream subtitling could be less concise and much more specific.

TABLE 6.9   Lost – *season 6, episode 1*

Original Dialogue – *Lost* season 6, episode 1	
Actually, in calm seas with a good pilot, we could survive a water landing.	

DVD Version	Back Translation
Sub 1 Se il mare fosse calmo e il pilota bravo,	If the sea was calm and the pilot good,
Sub 2 potremmo <u>farcela</u> in realtà.	**we could make it**, actually.

ItaSA's Version	Back Translation
Sub 1 Veramente, <u>in acque calme</u>	Actually, **in calm seas**
Sub 2 e con un buon pilota, potremmo <u>sopravvivere a un ammaraggio.</u>	and with a good pilot, we could **survive a water landing.**

Subsfactory's Version	Back Translation
Sub 1 In realtà, <u>con mare calmo,</u>	Actually, **with calm sea**
Sub 2 e un buon pilota potremmo <u>sopravvivere all'ammaraggio.</u>	and a good pilot, we could **survive the water landing.**

In the original dialogue two characters on the plane talk about the possibility of a plane crash: "Actually, in calm seas with a good pilot, we could survive a water landing". The DVD version shows an oversimplified rendering, even if the number of characters available allow for a complete translation (back translation: "if the sea was calm and the pilot good, we could make it, actually"). As shown in the table, the subtitlers who produced the DVD version have plenty of space available for a complete rendering in order to convey the equivalent of "water landing" into the target language, yet we witness an inadvertent inaccuracy here. On the other hand, the versions produced by Subsfactory and ItaSA allow for a complete translation of the source text; while the latter is lacking in fluency (the expression "in acque calme", in fact, sounds like a translation), the version offered by Subsfactory ("con mare calmo") is of a better quality and more fluent in the target language.

Sometimes, however, "extreme condensation" is not only necessary, but is also advisable. The following scene (see Table 6.10), in which the characters are arguing about a bomb that went off and was supposed to change the course of time, shows how a sequence of two subtitles can be merged in Italian, and transformed into a single sentence.

DOI: 10.1057/9781137470379.0010

TABLE 6.10   Lost – *season 6, episode 1*

Original Dialogue – *Lost* season 6, episode 1
Sub 1   You said we could stop it from ever being built!
Sub 2   That our plane would have never crash on this land.

DVD Version	Back Translation
Sub 1 Dicevi che impedendone la costruzione,	You said that, avoiding the construction, the plane wouldn't have crashed on the island!
Sub 2 l'aereo non si sarebbe schiantato sull'isola.	

ItaSA's Version	Back Translation
Sub 1 Avevi detto che avremmo potuto evitare che venisse costruita.	You said that we could have prevented that it was built
Sub 2 così il nostro aereo non sarebbe mai precipitato su quest'isola.	so that our plane would have never crashed on this island.

Subsfactory's Version	Back Translation
Sub 1 Avevi detto che avremmo potuto impedire che venisse costruita.	You said that we could have avoided that it was built
Sub 2 Che il nostro aereo non si sarebbe mai schiantato su quest'isola.	so that our plane would have never crashed on this island.

The source text is composed of the following sentences: "You said we could stop it from ever being built!", and "that our plane would have never crash on this land". In the DVD we find the following rendering: "Dicevi che impedendone la costruzione,//l'aereo non si sarebbe schiantato sull'isola", (back translation: "You said that, avoiding the construction//the plane wouldn't have crashed on the island!"). Professionals here, have chosen to adopt the strategy of nominalisation converting the verb "built" into the Italian noun "costruzione" ("building"), thus considerably reducing and condensing the source dialogue. On the other hand, both fansubbed versions are rather literal, in accordance with established fansubbing guidelines which aim for an extremely faithful rendering of the source text. Similarly, fidelity to the source text can also mean rendering nuances of the audiovisual product style, such as informal and foul language as in the following scene (Table 6.11).

As we can see, Subsfactory renders the source text expression "get your asses" with the quite literal "portate il culo", while in the DVD all the traces of foul language are omitted and the translation reads: "come

TABLE 6.11   Lost – *season 6, episode 1*

Original Dialogue – *Lost* season 6, episode 1	
Get your asses to international Baggage Claim. We've got a 341.	
DVD Version	**Back Translation**
<u>Venite subito</u> al <u>Reclamo Bagagli</u>. Abbiamo un 341.	**Come immediately** to the **Complaint Baggage Office**. We've got a 341.
Subsfactory's Version	**Back Translation**
<u>Portate il culo</u> all'<u>area ritiro bagagli</u> internazionali. Abbiamo un 341.	**Get your asses** to international **Baggage Claim**. We've got a 341.

immediately". Unfortunately, and to the TV show's detriment, foul language is often censored in professional versions (see Chapter 7, which focuses on humour and censorship). Incidentally, in this subtitle, apart from the issue of censorship, we can discern a significant mistranslation on the part of professional subtitlers of the term "baggage claim". In airports, a "baggage claim" is an area where passengers can claim their luggage after disembarking from the aeroplane. In the Italian version, "baggage claim" becomes "reclamo bagagli" (back translation, "complaint baggage office") where "claim" acts as a false friend. Interestingly, Subsfactory produces a perfect translation of the expression, rendering it as "area ritiro bagagli".

Another case of omission relating to slang is displayed in the source language sentence: "That sucks!" which becomes "It's terrible!" in Italian (Table 6.12).

Once again, both fansubbing communities offer a translation that does not level down the language or suppress the original meaning, by using an appropriate equivalent and an adequate register in the target text: "Che sfiga!" (back translation: "what bad luck!").

In the final example an interesting case relating to the translation of the word "walkabout" is introduced. On the plane two characters are engaged in a conversation in which one of them asks the other the reason for his trip to Australia; the other character replies that he went there for a "walkabout". The other goes on to ask: "Like Crocodile Dundee?", in an attempt to specify the kind of activity implied (back translation: "Tipo Crocodile Dundee?"). What seems strange here is that in all the versions

DOI: 10.1057/9781137470379.0010

TABLE 6.12   Lost – *season 6, episode 1*

Original Dialogue – *Lost* season 6, episode 1	
Sorry, dude. That sucks.	
DVD Version	**Back Translation**
Mi dispiace, <u>è terribile</u>.	I'm sorry, **it's terrible**.
Subsfactory's Version	**Back Translation**
Mi spiace, bello. <u>Che sfiga</u>.	I'm sorry, handsome. **What bad luck**.
ItaSA's Version	**Back Translation**
<u>Che sfiga</u>, coso. Mi spiace.	**What bad luck**, thing. I'm sorry.

TABLE 6.13   Lost – *season 6, episode 1*

Original Dialogue – *Lost* season 6, episode 1	
Actually, I went on a walkabout.	
DVD Version	**Back Translation**
A fare una <u>walkabout</u>.	To have a **walkabout**.
Subsfactory's Version	**Back Translation**
Per la verità sono andato a fare un <u>walkabout</u>.	Actually, I went to have a **walkabout**.
ItaSA's Version	**Back Translation**
In realtà ero andato a fare un <u>walkabout</u>.	Actually, I went to have a **walkabout**.

produced, both fansubbed and professional, the term "walkabout" has been left untranslated (see Table 6.13).

In Australian English, a "walkabout" is a "temporary return to traditional aboriginal life, taken especially between periods of work or residence in modern society and usually involving a period of travel through the bush".[1] It could also indicate a simple walking trip, or a short leave of absence from work. In all these cases, the average viewer would probably not understand the exact meaning of the word without an adequate translation. Yet, the reasons behind this choice become clear if we bear in mind the fansubbing behaviours analysed so far, to convey a sense of otherness, for instance. However, this does not explain the

DOI: 10.1057/9781137470379.0010

decision to adopt a borrowing for this term on the part of the professional subtitlers.

The examples included here are not meant to denigrate professional translators. On the contrary, they merely highlight the fact that not all amateur translators are as bad as is commonly thought. It is the aim of this book to emphasise the fact that audiovisual translation in general should be taken more seriously and involve recommended and qualified professionals, instead of relying on "cheap alternatives". Hence, all things considered, the behaviour of fansubbers is not arbitrary; on the contrary, their faithfulness to the source text is a regular trait in their approach to translation, and as we have shown in the cases cited above, it can lead to a positive outcome as far as the expression of style and register are concerned.

6.3   Typographical conventions

In Chapter 4, the topic of norms has been dealt with fairly extensively. This section includes an analysis of the different treatment of punctuation conventions in professional subtitling and fansubbing. As far as punctuation is concerned, subtitling standards employ italics, "to indicate an off-screen source of the spoken text" (Karamitroglou 1998:2). In the scene below, we find one of the leading characters, Jack Shepard, in an airport listening to an announcement over the loud speakers (Table 6.14).

TABLE 6.14   Lost – *season 6, episode 1*

Original Dialogue – *Lost* season 6, episode 1	
Oceanic passenger Jack Shephard, Jack Shephard, please go to the nearest courtesy desk.	
DVD Version	**Back Translation**
Il signor Jack Shephard è pregato di recarsi al banco Oceanic.	Mr Jack Shephard please go to the Oceanic desk.
Subsfactory's Version	**Back Translation**
Sub 1 Il passeggero della Oceanic, Jack Shephard. **Sub 2** e' pregato di recarsi all'assistenza clienti piu' vicina.	Oceanic passenger Jack Shephard, please go to the nearest courtesy desk.

DOI: 10.1057/9781137470379.0010

While in the DVD version, the subtitles make use of italics to highlight the fact that the voice comes from an electronic device, in the version fansubbed by Subsfactory, no such differentiation is made. When using Subtitle Workshop, subbers can easily switch the typographical font from normal to italics by simply adding the tag "<i>" at the beginning of the subtitle.

The use of italics for the same purposes as in professional subtitling is established in both ItaSA and Subsfactory's guidelines, yet, after analysing a large number of versions in order to map out the frequency of italics in fansubbing, the conclusion has been reached that its use is relatively rare and is limited to the translation of specific genres, (British and period dramas, for example). This typographical font seems to be used more to highlight an anachronistic style rather than a contemporary one. In this case, the fact that the voice speaking does not belong to one of the characters on screen is quite straightforward, suggesting that subbers might have thought it unnecessary to stress the difference.

We should now address the question of how fansubbing has evolved over time. Apart from the fact that the constant and disproportionate faithfulness to the original dialogues has remained unchanged, there are a number of other changes, notably that the fansubbed versions relating to the sixth and final season of *Lost* do not show the same cases of mistranslation or lack of comprehension and misinterpretation observed during the second season. Indeed, the fact that the number of characters established in the fansubbing guidelines is religiously followed and in general the cps are respected, means that, not only are amateur translations of a better quality, but clearly the cueing process has also attained a standard of excellence. Thus, even if some subtitles might ideally be more condensed and concise, the translation is of a good quality and at times the choices made for the adaptation are far better than the version produced on DVD. This would indicate that an evolution has taken place within these communities over time, not only in terms of language proficiency, but also in terms of artistic expression and creativity, aspects frequently marginalised by professional subtitling.

We might conclude by asking how dissimilar professional and fansubbed versions are one from the other. Apart from a set of accidental misprints, for example the use of commas before the conjunction "e" (and) in Italian, the excessive faithfulness to the dialogue, which often leads to the imitation of the same syntactic structures and calques in the target language, as well as a number of cumbersome syntactic

DOI: 10.1057/9781137470379.0010

and semantic segmentations, it is impossible to pinpoint any appreciable difference between the official and the fansubbed versions. On the contrary, the DVD version appears to have been influenced by the work of the amateurs, even if it is then refined, embellished and finally polished for publication.

Apart from the differences noted above, after a careful analysis of the three versions, (the DVD, ItaSA and Subsfactory's), on the whole there is the sense that the work of professionals is frequently the result of the best of both fansubbed products, since many renderings, adaptation and solutions resemble those published by amateur translators too closely. Therefore, all the evidence suggests that fansubbing – since it is online, free and available – provides a convenient source for translation rough drafts containing ideas, tips and hints, from which professionals can draw liberally at anytime. Unfortunately, this sort of "legal plagiarism" can be clearly perceived throughout the episodes analysed. The work of amateur translators seems to be better than might be expected, not only for professional subtitlers who exploit it, but also in terms of financial gain for subtitling companies which are able to rely on simply proofreading free translations. According to Vellar, "Italian professionals started to capitalize on the skills of fansubbers to produce professional content without always acknowledging their contribution" (2011:5). In times like these, with the global financial crisis and all its consequences, subtitling rates have been consistently lowered, a fact which has led companies to hire inexperienced, unqualified translators who are willing to accept inadequate rates, while experienced subtitlers are turning to other markets in which to make a living. Fansubbers play an important role in this respect and, if they were to realise how crucial their co-creative labour is to the subtitling industry, they might hold the key to great change.

Note

1 As defined by www.thefreedictionary.com.

DOI: 10.1057/9781137470379.0010

7
Censorship and Humour in *Californication*

Abstract: *This section focuses on the topic of censorship associated with the expression of humour in the TV show* Californication. *It begins, firstly, by investigating a set of examples followed by an analysis of cases based on instances of mistranslation and undertranslation as far as adaptation is concerned, due to the misinterpretation of slang terms on the part of both fansubbers and professionals. It goes on, secondly, to analyse the adaptation of politically incorrect content by employing a set of cases from the pilot episode of* Californication. *The leitmotiv of this chapter involves the irredeemable inability of mainstream subtitling to produce an adequate output in terms of adherence to the original. The manner in which fansubbing manages to restore the humorous effect of the original dialogue is also demonstrated.*

Massidda, Serenella. *Audiovisual Translation in the Digital Age: The Italian Fansubbing Phenomenon.* Basingstoke: Palgrave Macmillan, 2015. DOI: 10.1057/9781137470379.0011.

DOI: 10.1057/9781137470379.0011

This section focuses mainly on the topics of censorship and manipulation associated with the expression of humour, external references and slang. It begins, firstly, by investigating a set of examples concerned with censorship and humour, followed by an analysis of cases based on specific instances of mistranslation and undertranslation as far as adaptation is concerned, due to the misinterpretation of external references, inside jokes and slang terms on the part of both fansubbers and professional translators. It goes on, secondly, to analyse the adaptation of politically incorrect content by employing a set of cases from the pilot episode of *Californication*. The leitmotiv of this chapter involves the irredeemable inability of mainstream subtitling to produce an adequate output in terms of adherence to the original. The manner in which fansubbing manages to restore the humorous effect of the original dialogue is also demonstrated.

In the translation of audiovisual products, the practice of censorship or the suppression of what might be perceived as offensive on many levels (e.g., foul language and explicit or inconvenient content), unfortunately still remains an unresolved issue in both dubbing and subtitling. The reason behind this peculiar attitude towards audiovisual translation is due to various factors: not only to distribution companies and the policies of public TV networks, "in order [for them] to adhere to what they consider politically correct" (Scandura 2004:1), but also, in the worst-case scenario it may derive from a process of self-censorship on the part of translators, who lack adequate knowledge of the foreign sub-culture and sub-language, which results in instances of undertranslation of which they are unaware. However, when we deprive an audiovisual text of the strong language used to express explicit references to sexual practices, the use of drugs and offensive or politically incorrect language, there might be a sense of semantic loss, especially when these references are not arbitrary, but strictly connected to the expression of word puns and humour in general. This is, in fact, the case with *Californication*.

Californication is a TV show created by Tom Kapinos and aired for the first time on Showtime in 2007. The series revolves around the main protagonist, Hank Moody (David Duchovny), a novelist *à la* Bukowski, who is involved in a complicated relationship with his long-standing girlfriend Karen (Natascha McElhone) and daughter Becca (Madeleine Martin). In the episode under analysis, we find him dealing with a writer's block as well as battling with his addictions to sex, drugs and alcohol, which are expressed in rather explicit language.

DOI: 10.1057/9781137470379.0011

In Italy, the pilot episode under analysis was broadcast on 6 March 2008 by the digital satellite pay TV Jimmy. ItaSA released the fansubs on 4 June 2008 at 23:15. The subtitled version analysed relates to the DVD distributed by Paramount Home Entertainment Italy, and released on 20 January 2009. The fact that the distribution company provided the translation without relying on the services of any subtitling firms has resulted in a low quality outcome, as is shown in detail in the following analysis.

7.1   Sex, humour and foul language

A scene in which we find the protagonist, Hank, in bed with a married woman is described in Table 7.1.

After having sex, the two characters are engaged in a conversation full of metaphors and references to erogenous body parts as the woman is

TABLE 7.1   Californication – *season 1, episode 1*

Original Dialogue – *Californication* season 1, episode 1	
Hank: Does he, you know, go downtown, tour the southland? **Woman:** Never **Hank:** Go under the hood? Near the yaganus?	

DVD Version	Back Translation
Hank: Si fa mai un giro da quelle parti, là in basso? **Woman:** Mai. **Hank:** Va mai nel boschetto? Vicino alla bernarda?	**Hank:** Does he tour the parts down there? **Woman:** Never **Hank:** Go under the **little hood**? Near the **bernarda**?

Subsfactory's Version	Back Translation
Hank: Lui non va mai giù in centro? Verso sud? **Woman:** Mai. **Hank:** Nella foresta? Vicino alla vagina?	**Hank:** Does he ever go downtown? Towards the South? **Woman:** Never **Hank:** In the **hood**? Near the **vagina**?

ItaSA's Version	Back Translation
Hank: Lui non va mai giù in centro? Verso sud? **Woman:** Mai. **Hank:** Nella foresta? Vicino all'altro buco?	**Hank:** Does he ever go downtown? Towards the South? **Woman:** Never **Hank:** In the **hood**? Near **the other hole**?

DOI: 10.1057/9781137470379.0011

complaining about the fact that her husband does not give her enough pleasure. As we can infer from the dialogue shown in the table, the exchange begins with a metaphor referring to the act of oral sex performed on a female, known as "cunnilingus", making use of imagery connected with "hoods" and "southlands". The tension builds up until Hank comes up with the neologism "vaganus", a combination of "vagina" and "anus" to refer to the area that contains both external openings. In the DVD, the translator employs the word "bernarda" to translate the English term, an old-fashioned expression that only refers to "vagina", toning down the strong sexual connotation of the source language and censoring the word "anus". Subsfactory simply chooses the easiest way by employing the neutral term "vagina", while once again omitting the reference to "anus". On the contrary, a more creative and complete translation is offered by ItaSA's subbers who manage to render all the references implied in the source text message by using a rather indirect style, "vicino all'altro buco?" (back translation: "near the other hole?"). It is worth noting that, in the dubbed version, "vicino all'ano?" (back translation: "near the anus?") is chosen, as described by Bucaria (2009) in her paper "Translation and censorship on Italian TV: an inevitable love affair".

We may assume that the DVD version may have censored the neologism, or worse, it could be a case of oversight on the part of the professionals. However, ItaSA at least has demonstrated a certain degree of creativity, aiming for more care and accuracy in their version.

In the scenes shown in Table 7.2, the conversation about sexual matters between the two characters continues, focusing on the exact position of the clitoris, as the woman's husband seems to have some issues finding it.

TABLE 7.2   Californication – *season 1, episode 1*

Original Dialogue – *Californication* season 1, episode 1	
I've stored it up my <u>ass.</u>	
DVD Version	**Back Translation**
Lo tenevo tra le <u>chiappe</u>.	I keep it **between my cheeks**.
Subsfactory's Version	**Back Translation**
Ce l'ho installato nel <u>culo</u>!	I've stored it up the **ass.**
ItaSA's Version	**Back Translation**
Piazzato nel <u>culo</u>, sì.	Stored up in the **ass**, yes.

DOI: 10.1057/9781137470379.0011

Making fun of this inexperienced man, Hunk says: "I just so happen to have my GPS with me. I've stored it up my ass". In this case, the focus of the analysis has been shifted from sexual innuendo to the translation of foul language. The term "ass" has a perfect and straightforward equivalent in Italian, "culo".

Once again, in the version on DVD, an edulcorated translation has been chosen, using the equivalent "chiappe" (back translation: "cheeks"), a term which is reminiscent of the archaic style of the word "bernarda" previously used (Table 7.1). In the dubbed version, the word "sedere" ("posterior") has been used, toning down the connotations of the source term even further. The inevitable consequence of mitigating the offensive language of the piece is that the style of the original dialogue is profoundly altered and the humour implicit in the strong words is instantly destroyed. Conversely, in the versions produced by both ItaSA and Subsfactory, the word "ass" has been translated by the direct Italian equivalent, "culo", maintaining the original atmosphere of the TV show.

As the scene goes on (see Table 7.3), the woman's husband comes back home and Hank tries to find somewhere to hide saying: "Well, maybe I should hide under your clit", making a reference to the previous scene when the woman said that her husband had no clue where her clitoris might be.

In the official version, "clit", the short, colloquial form of "clitoris" is translated by "vulva". We should now turn to a comparison of the two terms. While the term "clitoris" is defined as "the female erogenous organ

TABLE 7.3   Californication – *season 1, episode 1*

Original Dialogue – *Californication* season 1, episode 1	
Ok, maybe I should hide under your clit.	
DVD Version	**Back Translation**
Forse dovrei nascondermi dietro la tua <u>vulva</u>.	Maybe I should hide behind your **vulva**.
Subsfactory's Version	**Back Translation**
Forse è meglio se mi nascondo sotto al tuo <u>clitoride</u>.	Maybe it is better if I hide under your **clit**.
ItaSA's Version	**Back Translation**
Forse dovrei nascondermi sotto il tuo <u>clitoride</u>.	Maybe I should hide under your **clit**.

DOI: 10.1057/9781137470379.0011

capable of erection under sexual stimulation (female homologue of the male penis)",[1] and hence openly related to sex, the term "vulva" is described as "the external female genitalia surrounding the opening to the vagina and that collectively consist of the labia majora, the labia minora, and the clitoris".[2] Linguistically speaking, we might say that the professionals have adopted a hypernym in order to suppress an overtly sexual content and express the same content by a more neutral solution. On the other hand, faithful to the source text as usual, fansubbers belonging to both ItaSA and Subsfactory, simply used "clitoride", the perfect equivalent of "clit".

The following example serves to introduce the topic of swearwords. Bucaria's study on translation and censorship on Italian TV clearly indicates that, as far as Italian dubbing is concerned,

> no recurring patterns indicating a specific rationale for the deletion or toning down of swearwords or other potentially disturbing elements seemed to emerge from the analysis, perhaps suggesting a certain level of arbitrariness in the translational choices.
>
> (2009:1)

It is suggested here that what is certainly true for dubbing can be also applied to subtitling.

Table 7.4, for example, constitutes just one of the number of cases of total omission of explicit words.

The offensive word is "fuck", extensively used throughout the programme and apt in terms of characterising the protagonist and the

TABLE 7.4   Californication – *season 1, episode 1*

Original Dialogue – *Californication* season 1, episode 1	
▸ Hey, what the <u>fuck</u> was that? ▸ That would be my husband.	

DVD Version	Back Translation
▸ Che è stato? ▸ Dev'essere mio marito.	▸ What was that? ▸ It must be my husband.

Subsfactory's Version	Back Translation
▸ Chi <u>cazzo</u> è? ▸ Dev'essere mio marito.	▸ What the **fuck** was that? ▸ It must be my husband.

ItaSA's Version	Back Translation
▸ Che <u>cazzo</u> era quello? ▸ Dev'essere mio marito.	▸ What the **fuck** was that? ▸ It must be my husband.

DOI: 10.1057/9781137470379.0011

style of the script. The situation in which Hank pronounces the sentence, "hey, what the fuck was that?" appears to be relatively critical, because he has just heard a noise meaning that the woman's husband is returning home and is about to find out that his wife has cheated on him. As shown in the table, the term in question creates a liberating and comic effect by releasing the anxiety building up inside the protagonist. The perfect Italian equivalent would be the vulgar term "cazzo", which was the choice adopted by both fansubbing communities. Needless to say, the word is deliberately omitted in the DVD version and the translation produced ended up neutralising the style with a simple "what was that?".

The Italian adaptation of the TV show and its reception by the Italian audience has been discussed in various blogs:[3] the sorely disappointed fans seem to agree on the fact that the dubbed version of their favourite programme is almost unrecognisable, at times outrageous, and in the end they suggest watching it in English to appreciate it to the fullest extent.

> La forza di questa serie televisiva [...] è la brillantezza dei dialoghi, che fa dimenticare l'assurdità di alcune situazioni, e per questo è consigliabile vederla in lingua originale perché con il doppiaggio italiano perde molto, soprattutto per quanto riguarda l'inventiva linguistica del nostro scrittore in materia di parolacce e vocabolario sessuale.[4]

The blogger explains that the show relies on provocative, smart exchanges made of neologisms, offensive and explicit language able to convey a humorous effect. However, these elements are completely missing in the Italian adaptation, and as a result, the show is perceived as extremely boring and rather dull (see Table 1.1, Chapter 1 on *The Big Bang Theory*).

Sometimes, rather than being deleted entirely, bad words are often toned down, but considerably toned down in the professional version, as in the following scene (Table 7.5), where "why the fuck" becomes "perché diamine" (back translation: "what on earth") in the DVD, while it is correctly rendered in both fansubbed versions.

This process of manipulating explicit language on the part of professional translators continues relatively arbitrarily throughout the whole episode, in which we find that "motherfucker" becomes "figlio di buona donna" (back translation "son of good woman"), instead of "figlio di puttana" (used by both communities) which is the literal translation of the original swearword (Table 7.6).

Similarly, the explicit slang term "dick" becomes "biscotto" (back translation: "biscuit") in the DVD, while it is rendered literally as "cazzo"

DOI: 10.1057/9781137470379.0011

TABLE 7.5   Californication – *season 1, episode 1*

Original Dialogue – *Californication* season 1, episode 1	
Why the fuck would you do something like that?	

DVD Version	Back Translation
Perché <u>diamine</u> l'hai fatto?	Why **on earth** did you do that?

Subsfactory's Version	Back Translation
Perché <u>cazzo</u> avresti fatto una cosa del genere?	Why the **fuck** would you do something like that?

ItaSA's Version	Back Translation
Perché cazzo faresti una cosa simile?	Why the **fuck** would you do something similar?

TABLE 7.6   Californication – *season 1, episode 1*

Original Dialogue – *Californication* season 1, episode 1	
Mortherfucker!	

DVD Version	Back Translation
Figlio di buona donna!	Son of good woman!

Subsfactory's Version	Back Translation
Figlio di puttana!	Son of a bitch!

ItaSA's Version	Back Translation
Figlio di puttana!	Son of a bitch!

by ItaSA and "uccello" (back translation: "bird", a slang word for "cazzo", but with a milder impact) by Subsfactory (Table 7.7).

Among other strongly edulcorated swearwords found on DVD, the terms: "asshole" and "dick", frequently rendered as "idiota" and "deficiente" (back translation "idiot" and "moron"), should be also highlighted; these appear, however, as "cazzone/coglione" (back translation "prick") in the fansubbed versions.

Yet, not only do bad words magically disappear becoming slight reproaches, but as we have observed in the previous scenes, every little

DOI: 10.1057/9781137470379.0011

TABLE 7.7   Californication – *season 1, episode 1*

Original Dialogue – *Californication* season 1, episode 1	
You are out there sticking your dick in anything that moves.	
DVD Version	**Back Translation**
Te ne sai lì a <u>inzuppare il biscotto</u> in qualsiasi cosa si muova.	You are there **dipping your biscuit** in anything that moves.
Subsfactory's Version	**Back Translation**
Te ne vai in giro e infili il tuo <u>uccello</u> in tutto ciò che si muove.	You are out there sticking your **bird** in anything that moves.
ItaSA's Version	**Back Translation**
Te ne vai in giro a infilare il <u>cazzo</u> in qualsiasi cosa si muova.	You are out there sticking your **dick** in anything that moves.

reference to male or female genitals is systematically omitted. This is the case of the source sentence in the following example (Table 7.8), "that's the look that shrivels me testes", which presents a metaphor that makes reference to male genitals, "testes", being a diminutive of testicles.

TABLE 7.8   Californication – *season 1, episode 1*

Original Dialogue – *Californication* season 1, episode 1	
That's the look that shrivels me testes.	
DVD Version	**Back Translation**
Quello è lo sguardo che mi <u>fa tremare</u>.	That's the look that **makes me shiver**.
Subsfactory's Version	**Back Translation**
È lo sguardo che mi fa <u>avvizzire le palle</u>.	It's the look that **shrivels my balls**.
ItaSA's Version	**Back Translation**
Quello è lo sguardo che mi <u>stritola i coglioni</u>.	That's the look that **squeezes my bollocks**.

In the table above, displaying the version on DVD, we can see that the reference in question is deleted, and the translation reads: "quello è lo

DOI: 10.1057/9781137470379.0011

sguardo che mi fa tremare" (back translation: "that's the look that makes me shiver"). Conversely, both Subsfactory and ItaSA have managed to keep the reference to "testicles", using an adequate register to render the humorous expression. Subsfactory has translated testicles as "palle" (back translation: "balls") and ItaSA has used "coglioni" which might be a little strong (back translation: "bollocks"), although they are both suitable equivalents.

7.2   Political correctness

In this section, the adaptation of politically incorrect content is analysed in the pilot episode of *Californication*. In the following example, Karen, Hank's ex-wife, teases him since he has appeared at her home without any trousers, after escaping from the woman's husband who had caught him in bed with his wife, comparing him to "a special-needs person that works at McDonalds". It is a relatively strong statement, as it is a joke with a direct reference to disabled people (see Table 7.9).

In the DVD, "special needs" is rendered as "con difficoltà di apprendimento" (back translation: "with different learning abilities"), which is a way to censor the original expression while losing the humour expressed in the metaphor. Subsfactory uses the expression "persone disabili" (back

TABLE 7.9   Californication – *season 1, episode 1*

Original Dialogue – *Californication* season 1, episode 1	
He's much like a special-needs person that works at McDonald's.	
DVD Version	**Back Translation**
Come una persona <u>con difficoltà di apprendimento</u> che lavora da McDonald's.	He's like a person with **different learning abilities** that works at McDonald's.
Subsfactory's Version	**Back Translation**
È più come una di quelle persone <u>bisognose</u> che lavorano da MacDonald.	He's more like one of those people **in need** that work at McDonald's.
ItaSA's Version	**Back Translation**
È più tipo quelle persone <u>disabili</u> che lavorano da MacDonald.	He's more like those **disabled** people that work at McDonald's.

DOI: 10.1057/9781137470379.0011

translation: "disabled people"), which is perfectly in keeping with their faithful approach to translation in general as well as quite appropriately retaining the humorous effect of the target text. ItaSA, on the other hand, has opted for "persone bisognose" ("people in need"), misconstruing the original reference and producing a mistranslation. As been shown above, politically incorrect language may address specific groups of people, although it can also be used to reflect a pronounced bias towards gender, sexual orientation, culture, policies, religions, ideologies and the use of drugs.

The example given in Table 7.10 relates to a scene where Hank and his ex-wife are having an argument.

The protagonist, commenting on a statement made by his ex-wife, says: "[...] then it's possible that you are higher than me right now". The problem revolves around the translation of the term "higher" in the three versions. The term in question, "higher", which would normally define a state of altered consciousness induced by the use of narcotics, in this particular instance, expresses the state of being out of one's mind. In the DVD, the metaphor disappears and "higher" is rendered as "più fuori" (back translation "crazier"), where the reference to drugs appears to be toned down and the general meaning altered in favour of a more politically correct reference to psychological issues. As usual, both fansubbing communities have opted for the more straightforward equivalent, the slang term "fatta" (back translation "stoned"), which conveys the exact intention of the original dialogue.

TABLE 7.10   Californication – *season 1, episode 1*

Original Dialogue – *Californication* season 1, episode 1	
...then it's possible that you are higher than me right now.	
DVD Version	**Back Translation**
...allora sei <u>più fuori</u> di me.	...then you are **crazier** than me.
Subsfactory's Version	**Back Translation**
Possibile che tu sia <u>più fatta</u> di me al momento.	It's possible that you are **higher** than me right now.
ItaSA's Version	**Back Translation**
Possibile che tu sia <u>più fatta</u> di me al momento.	It's possible that you are **higher** than me right now.

DOI: 10.1057/9781137470379.0011

7.3   Adaptation and mistranslation

The leitmotiv of this chapter, which focuses on manipulation and its consequences, especially when it comes to the expression of humorous content, involves the irredeemable incapacity of mainstream subtitling to produce an adequate output in terms of faithfulness to the source text and adherence to the original style. The manner in which fansubbing manages to restore the original dialogues, attempting to produce faithful versions of the foreign product with excellent results has also been demonstrated. Apart from the topic of the censorship of offensive language, we have found that in the episode analysed, professional subtitlers sometimes produced a series of mistranslations totally unrelated to the expression of explicit language.

The following example (Table 7.11) shows how the source sentence expression "quid pro quo" is rendered in the three versions.

In the dialogue shown in the table, we can see that in the DVD version the sentence has been left almost untranslated: "qui pro quo". At this point, the meaning of the expression under analysis should be explained. "Quid pro quo" in English is used to convey the Latin phrase meaning "something for something". In fact, the woman is telling Hank that "you're nice to me, I'm nice to you". In Italian, the same sentence has a rather different meaning, since it equates to another Latin sentence, "do ut des" (back translation: "I give so that you will give"). Conversely, a "qui pro quo" in Italian defines a misunderstanding, or the substitution of one thing for another. Hence, while the professional subtitlers seem

TABLE 7.11   Californication – *season 1, episode 1*

Original Dialogue – *Californication* season 1, episode 1	
Yes, it's very quid pro quo.	
DVD Version	**Back Translation**
Beh, è un po' <u>qui pro quo</u>.	Well, it's a little **misunderstanding**.
Subsfactory's Version	**Back Translation**
Sì, è un vero qui <u>pro quo</u>.	Yes, it's a real **misunderstanding**.
ItaSA's Version	**Back Translation**
Oh, questo è molto <u>do ut des</u>.	Oh, this is very **quid pro quo**.

DOI: 10.1057/9781137470379.0011

to have completely misunderstood the actual meaning of the source sentence, at least one of the two fansubbing communities produced a good translation of the expression. In this case, ItaSA used "do ut des", while Subsfactory made the same mistake as in the DVD version.

The next example focuses on the adaptation of slang expressions. The source sentence, "Are you still feeling cute?" is uttered by Hank's ex-wife as a response to his nonchalant behaviour after his daughter has found a naked woman in her father's house. In the DVD the translation reads: "Hai ancora voglia di scherzare?" (Table 7.12).

The style used in the source sentence is quite informal, as Karen is trying to mock Hank by questioning his nonchalance. The verb "scherzare" (joke) in Italian is neither informal nor does it have any specific connotations, hence we might categorise it as constituting another case of undertranslation, since it does not manage to convey either the register or the humour of the original. On the other hand, in both fansubbed versions the English expression has been translated by "Fai ancora/ti senti ancora figo?", where "figo" is a literal equivalent of "cute", hence a perfect translation solution in terms of register and accuracy.

Throughout the whole show, there is only a single case in which the DVD version shows a better adaptation of a slang term than the fansubbed outcome. In the scene analysed (Table 7.13), Hank and his ex-wife are having an argument based on their past relationship, when a slang term comes up: "googling".

The humorous sentence reads: "sitting there, googling yourself". In Italian there is an equivalent expression, "googlare", a neologism derived

TABLE 7.12   Californication – *season 1, episode 1*

Original Dialogue – *Californication* season 1, episode 1	
Are you still feeling cute?	
DVD Version	**Back Translation**
Hai ancora voglia di <u>scherzare</u>?	Do you still feel like **joking**?
Subsfactory's Version	**Back Translation**
Ti senti ancora <u>figo</u>?	Are you still **feeling cute**?
ItaSA's Version	**Back Translation**
Fai ancora il <u>figo</u>?	Are you **acting cute**?

DOI: 10.1057/9781137470379.0011

TABLE 7.13   Californication – *season 1, episode 1*

Original Dialogue – *Californication* season 1, episode 1	
...sitting there, googling youself?	
DVD Version	**Back Translation**
...uno che stava lì a "<u>googlare</u>" il suo nome.	...one sitting there, **googling his name.**
Subsfactory's Version	**Back Translation**
...seduto lì, <u>cercando te stesso su Google.</u>	...sitting there, **looking for yourself** on Google.
ItaSA's Version	**Back Translation**
...seduto lì a <u>cercarti su Google.</u>	...sitting there, **looking for yourself** on Google.

from "Google", the name of the browser. This time, it was only the official translation that opted for the perfect and most commonly used equivalent, while both communities used "cercarti su google" (back translation: "looking for yourself on Google").

The most interesting example of mistranslation in the entire episode of *Californication* is illustrated in the following example (Table 7.14).

There is an ongoing discussion between the two characters and Karen makes another remark concerning Hank's flaws: "you've always been a walking id, Hank". The rendering of this sentence presents a set of challenges: first of all, the meaning of "id" in the context; secondly, its contextualised meaning associated with the adjective "walking". In the DVD version, the Italian subtitle reads: "sei sempre stato un "id" ambulante", which is the literal translation, and appears rather awkward since it has no meaning in the target language and resembles a fansubbed version rather than a professional one. The term "id", as defined by the *Encyclopaedia Britannica*, is related to Freudian psychoanalytic theory: it is the oldest of the three psychic realms – ego, superego and id – and the one containing "a set of uncoordinated instinctual drives".[5] The Italian equivalent of "id" is "es", the more widespread translation of the term found in the majority of books published on the topic. Yet, when it comes to the collocation of this term with the adjective "walking", another issue arises, since the meaning of the sentence changes. The subbers from

DOI: 10.1057/9781137470379.0011

TABLE 7.14   Californication – *season 1, episode 1*

Original Dialogue – *Californication* season 1, episode 1	
You've always been a walking id, Hank	
DVD Version	**Back Translation**
Sei sempre stato un "<u>id</u>" ambulante, Hank.	You've always been a **walking id**, Hank.
Subsfactory's Version	**Back Translation**
Sei sempre stato un <u>Es con le gambe</u>, Hank.	You've always been an **Es with legs**, Hank.
ItaSA's Version	**Back Translation**
Sì, sei sempre stato una mina vagante, Hank.	You've always been a **loose cannon**, Hank

Subsfactory attempted to adapt it by using the sentence "sei sempre stato un Es con le gambe", which is still quite literal, but at least shows a certain degree of elaboration since it provides a metaphor in which the "id" ("es") has legs ("gambe"). Conversely, the fansubbers from ItaSA, demonstrably understand the real meaning of the source text and have attempted to use the strategy of explicitation to make it comprehensible to the viewer: "sei sempre stato una mina vagante, Hank" (back translation "you've always been a loose cannon, Hank").

In the following scene (Table 7.15), the dialogue continues and Hank replies to Karen: "Hardly. More like a one-hit wonder".

The adaptation of "one-hit wonder", presents another case of mistranslation in the DVD version that reads: "una stella cadente". The source term expression refers to Hank's job as a writer who has published a bestseller, and now cannot seem to produce a single sentence, since he is suffering from writer's block. Thus, he considers himself to be a person who has enjoyed only one single success in his life. "Una stella cadente" is a "shooting star" in English, therefore there is no relation between the DVD subtitles and the original dialogue. Both Subsfactory and ItaSA translated the expression as "uno da una botta e via" (back translation "a man for a one-night stand") altering the initial meaning by changing the metaphor for a sexual innuendo. However, their version is a good attempt at conveying the meaning of the source expression, which in Italian should be "una meteora" to describe someone known just for one single success and that afterwards disappears from the scenes forever.

DOI: 10.1057/9781137470379.0011

TABLE 7.15   Californication – *season 1, episode 1*

Original Dialogue – *Californication* season 1, episode 1	
Hardly. More like a one-hit wonder.	
DVD Version	**Back Translation**
Non proprio. Più che altro una <u>stella cadente</u>.	Not really. More like a **shooting star.**
Subsfactory's Version	**Back Translation**
Non proprio. Più <u>uno da una botta e via</u>.	Not really. More **a man for a one-night stand.**
ItaSA's Version	**Back Translation**
A mala pena. Sono uno da una botta e via.	Hardly. More **a man for a one-night stand.**

7.4 Concluding remarks

A set of findings from the analysis of the pilot episode of *Californication* has revealed that the official translation found in the DVD version display a range of undertranslations due to various factors. Initially, as described in the first section, it was found that there was a tendency of professional subtitlers to tone down and often delete possible references to sex-related content – images connected to body parts and sexual acts – as well as offensive content (swearwords of different levels of intensity). Therefore, the consistent presence of diverse forms of manipulation has led professional subtitlers to produce poor quality translations in terms of faithfulness to the source text language and style. Moreover, this "censoring behaviour", whether intentional or not – since no specific pattern was found to explain the deletion of disturbing elements – destroyed the humour inherent in the very censored terms which were removed, creating a totally different product, which became mostly dull, neutralised and almost unrecognisable.

Yet, censorship may be a plausible justification for certain types of undertranslation, but as was shown in the second section which focused on adaptation and mistranslation, it cannot explain the inadequate renderings of the original text made by the professionals throughout the whole episode. We might, of course, accept such erratic and unpredictable behaviour if it had been found in the translation carried out by fansubbers,

DOI: 10.1057/9781137470379.0011

but we would certainly not expect this level of inaccuracy on the part of professional translators.

On the other hand, the tendency among fansubbers to adhere to the source text strictly, has proved ultimately successful, since for each mistranslation or understranlation found in the official subtitled version, a good equivalent and an adequate rendering of style and register were offered in one or both fansubbed versions under analysis. In conclusion, even if they were not absolutely perfect, the fansubbed versions managed to retain the humour, style, register and core message of the foreign audiovisual product, a rather unpredictable outcome for which we were unprepared during the first stages of the study.

Notes

1   www.britannica.com/search?query=clitoris.
2   www.britannica.com/search?query=vulva.
3   www.italiansubs.net/forum/person-of-interest/doppiaggio-italiano-95716/.
    www.subsfactory.it/forum/index.php?action=printpage;topic=6369.0.
    www.hwupgrade.it/forum/archive/index.php/t-1712862.html.
4   www.osservatoriesterni.it/schede/californication-serie-tv.
5   www.britannica.com/EBchecked/topic/281641/id.

DOI: 10.1057/9781137470379.0011

Conclusions: A Step into the Future

Massidda, Serenella. *Audiovisual Translation in the Digital Age: The Italian Fansubbing Phenomenon*. Basingstoke: Palgrave Macmillan, 2015. DOI: 10.1057/9781137470379.0012.

It has been mentioned repeatedly throughout this book, that the Italian fansubbing phenomenon today owes much to the TV show *Lost*. Seen from the perspective of Media Studies, *Lost* "has demonstrated a tremendous ability to encourage almost unprecedented viewer involvement and commitment both in form and degree" (Askwith 2007:152). After its conclusion, many publications on the TV show followed, and among them, one of the most recent, written by De Marco (2012) defines the popular programme with one, unique adjective, "total":

> *Lost* è una serie televisiva innovativa, rivoluzionaria, contemporanea. Ma prima di tutte queste cose è un telefilm totale, perché in esso è stato rappresentato il "tutto", relativamente a quel che concerne l'esistenza umana: ogni aspetto, ogni eventualità, ogni dubbio che l'umana condizione può sperimentare è stato messo in scena sull'Isola e fuori dall'Isola. E di fronte alla grandezza imponente del "tutto", l'uomo non può che sentirsi totalmente smarrito.

(2012:1–2)

If we paraphrase the author, we can confirm that *Lost* is indeed innovative, revolutionary and contemporary since it represents the human condition to its fullest with every tiny aspect, feeling, doubt and event within human existence being entirely covered in the polyphonic narrative and, as a consequence, the concept of "totality", as expressed by De Marco aptly describes life on the desert island. Men can only feel lost and insignificant in the face of this glorious power of totality.

We might ascribe the origin of what has been described as "the golden age of American TV shows" to the series *Lost*. During the last decade, US TV productions have shifted from a more traditional approach to a brand new category of series format, investing large amounts of money in ambitious projects created by famous producers and directors such as Martin Scorsese (HBO's *Boardwalk Empire*, for example), based on excellent scripts (FX's *Fargo* written by the Coen brothers, for example) and showing an incredible number of actors "stolen" from the cinema industry: Steve Buscemi (starring in *Boardwalk Empire*), Woody Harrelson and Matthew McConaughey, (starring in *True Detective*), Kevin Spacey and Robin Wright (*House of Cards*), just to name a few.

According to *The Hollywood Reporter*,[1] while, on the one hand, 144 original TV series were broadcast in 2013, on the other, the cinema industry is currently suffering a serious setback. Thus, in such a flamboyant era, it is no wonder that the potential value of the viewer's engagement with television, "the larger system of material, emotional, intellectual, social and psychological investments a viewer forms through their interactions with the expanded television text" (Askwith 2007:154), plays a substantial role in the development of fan translation in general and fansubbing in particular.

The fundamental purpose of this research was to understand if, and to what extent, the phenomenon of amateur translation has had an impact on audiovisual translation modes of transfer in Europe and Italy in particular. To this end, the wider implications of the practices of amateur experts on audiovisual translation studies have been observed in two major "historical" events.

In this book, we have described the case of *The Big Bang Theory*: the reaction to the airing of the dubbed episodes on the part of the fans, who had been following the show since 2007 thanks to fansubbers, was immediate and relatively harsh. Owing to the "italianisation" of the dubbed version, the nerdy-related content, which characterised the programme, was dumbed down; the adaptation had levelled down the language to such an extent that it did not appeal at all to the target audience who criticised the work of the dubbing company. Eventually, the controversy, which sparked several online blogs, led to dramatic changes to the dubbed production. Thus, the effective resistance of the active Italian audience made it clear that the patronising authority of the dubbing tradition was losing its grip in Italy.

The second crucial moment in the history of the Italian fansubbing phenomenon came in 2010, when for the very first time the final episode of *Lost* was aired simultaneously by a large number of pay-TV channels worldwide. In Italy, the episode was fansubbed by ItaSA and Subsfactory just a few hours after it had been aired in its original version; it was then re-aired by Sky Italia 24 hours later with Italian "pro-subtitles" and eventually broadcast after seven days in its dubbed Italian version. Never before had Italians witnessed such speed in dealing with audiovisual translation, and it is no wonder that the Italian fansubbing movement paved the way for this to happen. In fact, in Italy the practice of speeding up the audiovisual translation process – as far as pay TV channels are concerned – has currently been consolidated, at least for some important TV shows such as *Grey's Anatomy*, for instance. In fact, following what we might define as "the great AVT turn of 2010", Sky Italia now provides the Italian subtitles for the show noted above after only 24 hours and the dubbed version only after seven days after the airing in the United States.

DOI: 10.1057/9781137470379.0012

As a matter of fact, the key-events described clearly illustrate the crucial role played by fan translation in the evolution of audiovisual practices in Italy.

While such an outcome might be further perfected – owing to the fact that subtitling practices are still criticised by the fans of TV shows for not preserving the authenticity of the original product – it is hopeful that it might pave the way for future experiments and innovations in the area relating to subtitling norms.

The issue of norms has been another relevant aspect examined in this study. In fact, having revealed a series of interesting aspects concerning fansubbing practices, the case studies presented in the final chapters might inspire future research leading to the development of new subtitling standards. A hybrid proposal has, therefore, been advanced in this study, deriving from what we have considered as a blending of the best resources offered by both subtitling and fansubbing codes of practice.

The research project, which was begun with the assumption that, owing to the amateur nature of their work, amateur experts would ultimately have a lot to learn from professional translators, eventually reached the opposite conclusion. In fact, despite their apparent naivety, fansubbers have proved, by challenging long-established, fixed rules, that their collective effort might be a source of inspiration for both academics and professionals, as well as a valuable contribution to the investigation of future subtitling norms, thus enriching the debate concerning the reshaping of subtitling norms underlying future audiovisual translation in Italy.

We have endeavoured to shed light on the grey area existing between piracy and promotion as well as the exploitation of digital labour so as to free fan translation from any accusations connected with copyright infringement as well as emphasising the social value of their unselfish, unpaid work.

Additionally, we have contextualised the phenomenon of fansubbing within the revolution brought about by Web 2.0, highlighting the fact that, while it has certainly favoured co-creational activities, it has also been exploited as a marketing tool by multinational companies such as Facebook, for example, in order to outsource translation projects to their users for free, thus creating "a hole" in the translation industry and harming professional translation.

In this book we have described a pioneering study on fansubbing, and, as a consequence, we are keenly aware that future research is needed

DOI: 10.1057/9781137470379.0012

in order to investigate more in depth aspects we could, unfortunately, not address in this monograph for purely practical reasons. The developmental pathways we expect academics working in a variety of fields to follow in the future are represented, firstly, by offering a clarification of the issue of copyright infringement as far as translation and the derivative works of fansubbers are concerned. Secondly, the question posed by "digital playbour" (Scholz) and the consequences caused by the exploitation of Internet users along with the precarious working balance of professionals, require analysis. Last, but not least, we consider a future investigation on the impact of fansubbing on the acquisition of a second language (English for the Italian audience, for example) on the part of the fansubbers themselves as well as users, to be of paramount importance. A study of this kind might be able to unveil whether and how a massive exposure to a cognitive learning method known as the "latent learning process" (cf. Tolman 1948; D'ydewalle and Pavakanun 1997) represented by a subterreanean, grassroots phenomenon such as fansubbing, and occurring in a semi-learning environment, has contributed to the linguistic learning process among foreign language learners and younger generations of TV show addicts in general.

Note

1   http://www.hollywoodreporter.com/.

DOI: 10.1057/9781137470379.0012

References

Anon. 2008. "Study on Dubbing and Subtitling Needs and
   Practices in the European Audiovisual Industry. *Media
   Consulting Group (MCG)*. www.lt-innovate.eu date
   accessed 18 November 2014.

Antonini, R. 2008. "The Perception of Dubbese: an
   Italian study". In Chiaro, D., Heiss C., Bucaria, C.
   (eds), *Between Text and Image: Updating Research in
   Screen Translation*. (Amsterdam & Philadelphia: John
   Benjamins), pp. 135–147.

Antonini, R. and Chiaro, D. 2009. "The Perception of
   Dubbing by Italian Audiences". In Díaz-Cintas, J. and
   Anderman, G. (eds), *Audiovisual translation: language
   transfer on screen*. (New York: Palgrave Macmillan),
   pp. 97–114.

Ascheid, A. 1997. "Speaking Tongues: Voice Dubbing
   in the Cinema of Cultural Ventriloquism". In *The
   Velvet Light Trap*, 40, pp. 32–41. www.kent.ac.uk/arts/
   film/filmcentre/materials/ascheid.pdf date accessed
   05/12/2013.

Askwith, I. D. 2007. "Television 2.0: Reconceptualizing
   TV as an Engagement Medium". *B.A. Thesis,
   Massachusetts Institute of Technology, Media & Culture.
   New York University*. http://cms.mit.edu/research/
   theses/IvanAskwith2007.pdf date accessed 9 July 2014.

Banks, J. and Deuze, M. 2009. "Co-creative Labour",
   International Journal of Cultural Studies, 12, pp. 419–431.

Barra, L. and Guarnaccia, F. 2009. "Un lavoro di squadra.
   Processi produttivi e organizzazione gerarchica dei
   fansubber", *Link. Idee per la televisione*, 6, pp. 243–251.

DOI: 10.1057/9781137470379.0012

Bassett, C. (2013), "Silence, Delirium, Lies", *First Monday*, 18, pp. 3–4.

Baym, N. 2010. *Embracing the Flow*. Research Memo, Convergence Culture Consortium, MIT. http://convergenceculture.org/research/c3-embracingflow-full.pdf date accessed 20 August 2014.

Baym, N. & Burnett, R. 2009. "Amateur Experts: International Fan Labor in Swedish Independent Music", *International Journal of Cultural Studies*. 12(5), pp. 433–449.

Beilby, D. et al. 1999. "Whose Stories Are They? Fans' Engagement with Soap Opera Narratives in Three Sites of Fan Activity", *Journal of Broadcasting & Electronic Media*, 43(1), reprinted in Miller, T. (ed.), *Television: Critical Concepts in Media and Cultural Studies* 2002. (New York: Routledge Press), pp. 35–51.

Bogucki, L. 2009. "Amateur Subtitling on the Internet". In: Díaz Cintas, J. and Anderman, G. (eds). *Audiovisual Translation: Language Transfer On Screen*. (London: Palgrave Macmillan).

Bold, B. 2012. "The Power of Fan Communities: an Overview of Fansubbing in Brazil", *Tradução em Revista*, 11, pp. 1–19.

Boyd, D. 2014. *It's Complicated: The Social Lives of Networked Teens*. (New Haven: Yale University Press).

Bruns, A. 2008. "The Future Is User-Led: The Path towards Widespread Produsage", *Fibreculture Journal* 11, pp. 1–10.

Bruti, S. and Zanotti, S. 2013. "Frontiere della traduzione audiovisiva: il fenomeno del fansubbing e i suoi aspetti linguistici". In Bosisio, C. and Cavagnoli, S. (eds), *Comunicare le discipline attraverso le lingue: prospettive traduttiva, didattica, socioculturale*, Atti del XII Congresso dell'Associazione Italiana di Linguistica Applicata. (Macerata, Perugia: Guerra Edizioni), pp. 119–142.

Bucaria, C. 2009. "Translation and Censorship on Italian TV: an Inevitable Love Affair?", *VIAL 6 - Vigo International Journal of Applied Linguistics, Special Issue on Translation and the Media* (R.A.Valdeón, ed). http://webs.uvigo.es/vialjournal/pdf/Vial-2009-Article1.pdf 13–32 date accessed 8 August 2014.

Bucaria, C. 2008. "Acceptance of the Norm or Suspension of Disbelief? The case of Formulaic Language in Dubbese". In Chiaro, D., Heiss C., Bucaria, C. (eds) *Between Text and Image: Updating Research in Screen Translation*. (Amsterdam & Philadelphia: John Benjamins), pp. 149–164.

Burwell, C. 2010. "Rewriting the Script: Toward a Politics of Young People's Digital Media Participation", *Review of Education, Pedagogy, and Cultural Studies*, 32:4–5, pp. 382–402.

DOI: 10.1057/9781137470379.0012

Caffrey, C. 2009. "Relevant Abuse? Investigating the Effects of an Abusive Subtitling Procedure on the Perception of TV Anime Using Eye Tracker and Questionnaire". (Doctoral thesis. Dublin: Dublin City University). http://doras.dcu.ie/14835/1/Colm_PhDCorrections. pdf date accessed 16 August 2014. C. Bazzanella (ed.). (Milano: Guerini), pp. 161–175.

Cantor, M. G. and Cantor, J. M. 1986. "Audience Composition and Television Content: The Mass Audience Revisited". In Ball-Rokeach, S. J. and Cantor, M. G. (eds), *Media, Audience, and Social Structure*. (Beverly Hills, CA: Sage), pp. 214–225.

Carroll, M. 2004. "Focus on Standards - Subtitling: Changing Standards for New Media", *The Globalisation Insider XIII, 3.3*. http://www. translationdirectory.com/article422.htm accessed 10 October 2013.

Casarini, A. 2014. "The Perception of American Adolescent Culture Through the Dubbing and Fansubbing of a Selection of US Teen Series from 1990 to 2013". (Doctoral thesis. Bologna: Alma Mater Studiorum – Università di Bologna).

Casarini, A. 2013. " 'You Have a Sarcasm Sign? Fansubbing and the Egalitarian Decryption of American Comedy". In Covi, G. and Marchi, L. (eds) *Democracy and Difference: the US in Multidisciplinary and Comparative Perspectives. Papers From the 2011 AISNA Conference*, (Trento: I Labirinti – Università di Trento).

Casarini, A. 2011. "Chorus Lines. Translating Musical TV Series in the Age of Participatory Culture: The case of *Glee*", *4th International Conference Media for All – Audiovisual Translation: Taking Stock*, London. (Unpublished).

Cate, A. C. 2009. "New Hollywood Narratives: an Analysis of Boogie Nights and Magnolia", *Honors Projects Overview. Paper 23*. http:// digitalcommons.ric.edu/honors_projects/23 date accessed 23 May 2013, pp. 1–48.

Chambers, S. 2012. "Anime: From Cult Following to Pop Culture Phenomenon". *The Elon Journal of Undergraduate Research in Communications*, 3(2), pp. 94–101.

Chaume, V. F. 2004. "Film Studies and Translation Studies: Two Disciplines at Stake in Audiovisual Translation", *Meta: Translators' Journal*, 49(1), pp. 12–24.

Chaume, V. F. 2004b. "Discourse Markers in Audiovisual Translating", *Meta*, 49 (4), pp. 843–855.

DOI: 10.1057/9781137470379.0012

Chesterman, A. 1998. "Description, Explanation, Prediction. A Response to Gideon Toury and Theo Hermans. In Schäffner, C, (ed.) *Translation and Norms*. (Clevedon: Multilingual Matters), pp. 91–98.

Chesterman, A. 1997. *Memes of Translation: The Spread of Ideas in Translation Theory*. (Amsterdam; Philadelphia: J. Benjamins).

Chesterman, A. 1993. "From 'Is' to 'Ought': Laws, Norms and Strategies in Translation Studies", *Target*, 5, pp. 1–27.

Chronin, M. 2013. *Translation in the Digital Age*. (London and New York, Routledge).

Chronin, M. 2010. "The Translation Crowd", *Revista Tradumàtica*, 8, pp. 1–7.

Cipolloni, M. 1996. "Il film d'autore e il doppiaggio". In Di Fortunato, E. and Paolinelli, M. (eds), *Barriere linguistiche e circolazione delle opere audiovisive: La questione doppiaggio.*(Roma: AIDAC), pp. 38–45.

Costello, V. and Moore, B. 2007. "Television Fandom Cultural Outlaws: An Examination of Audience Activity and Online", *Television & New Media*, 8 (2), pp. 124–143.

Danan, M. 1991. "Dubbing as an Expression of Nationalism", *Meta: Translators' Journal*, 36(4), pp. 606–614.

D'Aversa, P. 1996. "Introduzione". In Di Fortunato, E. and Paolinelli, M. (eds), *Barriere linguistiche e circolazione delle opere audiovisive:La questione doppiaggio.* (Roma: AIDAC).

De Kosnik, A. 2013. "Interrogating 'Free' Fan Labor". In Jenkins, H., Ford, S. and Green, J. (eds) *Spreadable Media: Creating Value and Meaning in a Networked Culture.* (New York: New York University Press). http://spreadablemedia.org/essays/kosnik/#.UbEevZzqOZQ date accessed 28 August 2014.

De Kosnik, A. 2012. "Fandom as Free Labor". In Scholz, T. (ed). *Digital Labor: The Internet as Playground and Factory*, pp. 98–111. (New York: Routledge).

De Linde, Z. and Kay, N. 1999. *The Semiotics of Subtitling*. (Manchester: Saint Jerome Publishing).

De Marco, M. 2012. *Totally Lost: Il libro definitivo sulla serie tv più amata*. (Bologna: Area51 Publishing).

Decrem, B. 2006. "Introducing Flock Beta 1", *Internet Archive Wayback Machine*. http://web.archive.org/web/20071024141305/http://flock.com/node/4500 date accessed 16 August 2014.

Delabastita, D. 1989. "Translation and Mass-Communication: Film and TV Translation as Evidence of Cultural Dynamics", *Babel*, 35(4), 193–218.

DOI: 10.1057/9781137470379.0012

Deuze, M. 2011. "Media Life", *Media Culture Society*, 33, pp. 137–149.

Deuze, M. 2007. "Convergence Culture in the Creative Industries", *International Journal of Cultural Studies*, 10, 2, pp. 243–263.

Díaz-Cintas, J. 2012. "Interview to Díaz-Cintas". In Anon. "Studies on Translation and Multilingualism: Crowdsourcing Translation", *European Commission, Directorate-General for Translation*, pp.65–72. http://ec.europa.eu/ date accessed 5 July 2014.

Díaz-Cintas, J. (ed.) 2008. *The Didactics of Audiovisual Translation*. (Amsterdam & Philadelphia: John Benjamins Publishing).

Díaz -Cintas, J. 2005. "Subtitles for Almodovar". *British Council Arts*.

Díaz-Cintas, J. 2003. *Teoría y Práctica de la Subtitulación: Inglés-Español*. (Barcelona: Ariel).

http://www.literarytranslation.com/workshops/almodovar accessed 5 December 2013.

Díaz-Cintas, J. 2001. *La Traducción Audiovisual: El Subtitulado*. (Salamanca: Almar).

Díaz-Cintas, J. and Remael, A. 2007. *Audiovisual Translation: Subtitling*. (Manchester: St. Jerome).

Díaz Cintas, J. and Muñoz Sánchez, P. 2006. "Fansubs: Audiovisual Translation in an Amateur Environment", *Jostrans: The Journal of Specialised Translation*, 6, pp. 37–52.

DiNucci, D. 1999. "Fragmented Future", *Print*, 32, pp. 220–222. www.darcyd.com/fragmented_future.pdf date accessed 1October 2014.

Dwyer, T. 2012. "Fansub Dreaming on ViKi "Don't Just Watch But Help When You Are Free", *The Translator: Non-Professionals Translating and Interpreting. Participatory and Engaged Perspectives*, pp. 217–243.

D'ydewalle, G. and Pavakanun, U. 1997. "Could Enjoying a Movie Lead to Language Acquisition?". In Winterhoff-Spurk, P. and Van der Voort, T. (eds), *New Horizons in Media Psychology*. (Opladen, Germany: Westdeutscher-Verlag GmbH), pp. 145–155.

D'ydewalle, G., and Gielen, I. 1992. "Attention Allocation with Overlapping Sound, Image, and Text". In Rayner, K. (ed.), *Eye Movements and Visual Cognition: Scene Perception and Reading*, (New York: Springer-Verlag), pp. 415–427.

D'ydewalle G., Praet C., Verfaillie K. and Van Rensbergen J. 1991. "Watching Subtitled Television. Automatic Reading Behaviour", *Communication Research*, 18(5), pp. 650–666.

D'ydewalle, G., Van Rensbergen J. and Pollet, J. 1987. "Reading a Message When the Same Message is Available Auditorily in Another

DOI: 10.1057/9781137470379.0012

Language: the Case of Subtitling". In O'Regan, J. K. and Lévy-Schoen, A. (eds) *Eye Movements: From Physiology to Cognition*. (Amsterdam and New York: Elsevier Science Publishers), pp. 313–321.

Eco, U. 1976. *A Theory of Semiotics*. (Indiana: Macmillan Press).

Fernández Costales, A. 2012. "Collaborative Translation Revisited: Exploring the Rationale and the Motivation for Volunteer Translation", *Forum - International Journal of Translation* 10(1), pp. 115–142.

Fernández Costales, A. 2011. "2.0: Facing the Challenges of the Global Era", *Tralogy* 4. http://lodel.irevuesist.fr/tralogy/index.php?id=120 date accessed 20 August 2014.

Ferrer Simó, M. R. 2005. "Fansubs y Scanlations: la Influencia del Aficionado en los Criterios Profesionales", *Puentes*, 6, pp. 27–43.

Filmer, D. A. 2011. "Translating Racial Slurs: a Comparative Analysis of Gran Torino Assessing Transfer of Offensive Language Between English and Italian", *Masters Thesis, Durham University*. http://etheses.dur.ac.uk/3337 date accessed 13 June 2014.

Fuchs, C. 2013. "Class and Exploitation on the Internet". In Scholz, T. (ed.) *Digital Labor. The Internet as Playground and Factory*, (New York: Routledge). pp. 211–224.

Galassi, G. G. 1996. "Introduzione". In Di Fortunato, E. and Paolinelli, M. (eds), *Barriere linguistiche e circolazione delle opere audiovisive:La questione doppiaggio.* (Roma: AIDAC), pp. 12–15.

Gambier, Y., Shlesinger, M., Stolze, R. (eds). 2007. *Doubts and Directions in Translation Studies*. (Amsterdam & Philadelphia: John Benjamins).

García, I. 2010. "The Proper Place of Professionals (and Non-Professionals and Machines) in Web Translation", *Revista Tradumàtica* 8. www.fti.uab.cat/tradumatica/revista date accessed 22 August 2014.

Gee, J. P. and Hayes, E. R. (2011). *Language and Learning in the Digital Age*. (New York, NY: Routledge).

Georgakopoulou, P. 2006. "Subtitling and Globalisation", *JoSTrans, The Journal of Specialised Translation*, 6, 115–120. www.jostrans.org/issue06/art_georgakopoulou.php date accessed 29 October 2014.

Georgakopoulou, P. 2003. "Reduction Levels in Subtitling. DVD Subtitling: a Compromise of Trends", *Doctoral Thesis, University of Surrey.* http://epubs.surrey.ac.uk/602/ date accessed 22 October 2014.

Gorlée, D. L. (1994). *Semiotics and the Problem of Translation: with Special Reference to the Semiotics of Charles S. Peirce*. (Amsterdam: Rodopi).

DOI: 10.1057/9781137470379.0012

Gottlieb, H. 1998. "Subtitling" in Baker, M. (ed.), *Encyclopedia of Translation Studies*. *(*London: Routledge), pp. 244–248.

Herbst, T. 1987. "A Pragmatic Translation Approach to Dubbing." *EBU Review – Programmes, Administration, Law,* 6, pp. 21–23.

Hermans, T. 1999. *Translation in Systems. Descriptive and System-Oriented Approaches Explained.* (Manchester: St. Jerome Publishing).

Hermans, T. 1996. "Norms and the Determination of Translation: a Theoretical Framework". In Álvarez, R. and Vidal, C.-Á. (eds), *Translation, Power, Subversion.* (Clevedon, England: Multilingual Matters), pp. 24–51.

Hermans, T. 1991. "Translational Norms and Correct Translations". In van Leuven-Zwart, K. and Naaijkens, T. (eds), *Translation Studies: the State of the Art.* (Amsterdam, Netherlands: Rodopi), pp. 155–170.

Holmes, J. S. 1972/1988. "The Name and Nature of Translation Studies". In Holmes, J. S. *Translated! Papers on Literary Translation and Translation Studies.* (Amsterdam: Rodopi), pp. 67–80.

House, J. 1981. *A Model for Translation Quality Assessment.* (Tübingen: Narr).

Howe, J. 2009. *Why the Power of the Crowd is Driving the Future of Business.* (New York: Three Rivers Press).

Howe, J. 2006. "The Rise of Crowdsourcing". *Wired,* 14(6), pp. 1–4. www.wired.com/wired/archive/14.06/crowds.html date accessed 09 June 2014.

Innocenti, V. and Maestri, A. 2010. "Il lavoro dei fan. Il fansubbing come alternativa al doppiaggio ufficiale in *The Big Bang Theory*". In *MM2010. Le frontiere del "popolare" tra vecchi e nuovi media. Media Mutations. Convegno internazionale di studi sull'audiovisivo.* http://amsacta.unibo.it date accessed 28 August 2014.

Ivarsson, J. 1992. *Subtitling for the Media: A Handbook of an Art.* (Stockholm: Transedit).

Ivarsson, J. and Carroll, M. 1998. *Subtitling.* (Simrishamn: TransEdit).

Jenkins, H. 2008.*Convergence Culture.* (New York: New York University Press).

Jenkins, H. 1992. *Textual Poachers: Television Fans & Participatory Culture. Studies in culture and communication.* (New York: Routledge).

Kapsaskis, D. 2011. "Professional Identity and Training of Translators in the Context of Globalisation: The Example of Subtitling", *The Journal of Specialised Translation,* 16. www.jostrans.org/issue16/art_kapsaskis.php date accessed 30 October 2014.

DOI: 10.1057/9781137470379.0012

Kapsaskis, D. 2008. "Translation and Film: on the Defamiliarizing Effect of Subtitles", *New Voices in Translation Studies* (4) *Special Conference Issue*, pp. 42–52.

Karamitroglou, F. 2000. *Towards a Methodology for the Investigation of Norms in Audiovisual Translation.* (Amsterdam and Atlanta, GA: Rodopi).

Karamitroglou, F. 1998. "A Proposed Set of Subtitling Standards in Europe". In *Translation Journal* 2(2). www.bokorlang.com/journal/04stndrd.htm date accessed 11 February 2013.

Kayahara, M. 2005. "The Digital Revolution: DVD Technology and the Possibilities for Audiovisual Translation Studies", *Jostrans: The Journal of Specialised Translation*, 3, pp. 64–74. http://www.jostrans.org/issue03/art_kayahara.pdf date accessed 22 August 2014.

Keen, A. 2007. *The Cult of the Amateur: How Today's Internet is Killing Our Culture.* (New York: Currency).

Kovačič, I. 1994. "Relevance as a Factor in Subtitling Reductions". In Dollerup, C. and Lindegaard, A. (eds) *Teaching Translation and Interpreting 2: Insights, Aims, Visions.* Amsterdam: John Benjamins), pp. 245–251.

Kovačič, I. 1991. "Subtitling and Contemporary Linguistic Theories". In Jovanovic, M. (ed.) *Translation, A creative Profession: Proceedings / XIII World Congress of FIT – Belgrade 10990* (Beograd: Prevodilac), pp. 407–417.

Kruger, H. 2001. "The Creation of Interlingual Subtitles: Semiotics, Equivalence and Condensation", *Perspectives Studies in Translatology,* 9(3), pp. 177–196.

Leadbeater, C. and Miller, P. 2004. *The Pro-Am Revolution.* (London:Demos).

Lee, H.-K. 2011. "Participatory Media Fandom: a Case Study of Anime Fansubbing", *Media, Culture & Society*, 33(8), pp. 1131–1147.

Lee, H.-K. 2009. "Manga Scanlation: Between Fan Culture and Copyright Infringement", *Media, Culture & Society*, 31(6), pp. 1011–1022.

Lee, H.-K and Bielby, D. 2010. "A life Course Perspective on Fandom", *International Journal of Cultural Studies*, 13, pp. 429–451.

Lefevere, A. 1977. *Translating Literature: The German Tradition from Luther to Rosenzweig.* (Assen: Van Gorcum).

Leonard, S. 2005. "Progress Against the Law: Anime and Fandom, with the Key to the Globalization of Culture", *International Journal of Cultural Studies*, 8(3), pp. 281–305.

DOI: 10.1057/9781137470379.0012

Leonard, S. 2004. "Progress Against the Law: Fan Distribution, Copyright, and the Explosive Growth of Japanese Animation". http://web.mit.edu/seantek/www/papers/progress—columns.pdf date accessed 03/04/2013.

Lessig, L. 2004. *Free Culture: How Big Media Uses Technology and the Law to Lock Down Culture and Control Creativity.* (New York: Penguin Press).

Lewis, P. E. 1985. "The Measure of Translation Effects". In Graham, J. F. (ed.). *Difference in translation.* (Ithaca: Cornell University Press), pp. 31–62.

Lovink, G. and Rash, M. (eds). 2013. *Unlike Us Readers: Social Media Monopolies and Their Alternatives.* (Amsterdam: Institute of Network Cultures).

Luyken, G. et al. 1991. *Overcoming Language Barriers in Television.* (Manchester: The European Institute for the Media).

Mackenzie, A. 2012. "More Parts Than Elements: How Databases Multiply. Environment and Planning D", *Society and Space,* 30(2), pp. 335–350.

Mangiron, C. and O'Hagan, M. 2013. *Game Localization: Translating for the Global Digital Entertainment Industry.* (Amsterdam: John Benjamins Publishing).

Minchinton, J. 1993. *Sub-Titling.* (Hertfordshire, England: Manuscript).

Napoli, P. 2010. "Revisiting 'Mass Communication' and the 'Work' of the Audience in the New Media Environment", *Media, Culture & Society,* 32, pp. 505–516.

Nord, C. 1997. *Translating as a Purposeful Activity.* (Manchester, England: St. Jerome).

Nord, C. 1991. "Scopos, Loyalty, and Translational Conventions", *Target,* 3(1), pp. 91–110.

Nornes, A. M. 1999. "For an Abusive Subtitling", *Film Quarterly* 52(3), pp. 17–33.

O'Hagan, M. 2014. "Fan Translation and Translation Crowdsourcing". Paper presented at *Multimedia Translation in the Digital Age Conference.* London - Europe House. www.europe.org.uk date accessed 20 August 2014.

O'Hagan, M. 2011a. (ed.). "Translation as a Social Activity. Community Translation 2.0", *Special issue of Linguistica Antverpiensia New Series - Themes in Translation Studies,* 10, pp. 1–7.

O'Hagan, M. 2011b. "Community Translation: Translation as a Social Activity and Its Possible Consequences in the Advent of Web 2.0 and

DOI: 10.1057/9781137470379.0012

Beyond", www.lans-tts.be/docs/lans10–2011-intro.pdf date accessed 15 August 2014.

O'Hagan, M. 2009. "Evolution of User-generated Translation: Fansubs, Translation Hacking and Crowdsourcing", *Journal of Internationalisation and Localisation*, 1(1), pp. 94–121.

O'Hagan, M. 2008. "Fan Translation Networks: an Accidental Translator Training Environment?". In Kearns J. (ed.) *Translator and Interpreter Training: Issues, Methods and Debates*, (London: Continuum), pp. 158–183.

O'Reilly, T. "What Is Web 2.0", http://oreilly.com/web2/archive/what-is-web-20.html date accessed 16 August 2014.

Orrego-Carmona, D. 2014a. "Subtitling, Video Consumption and Viewers: The Impact of the Young Audience", *Translation Spaces 3*, pp. 51–70.

Orrego-Carmona, D. 2014b. "Where Is the audience? Testing the Audience Reception of Non-professional Subtitling". In *Translation Research Projects 5*, Torres-Simon, E. and Orrego-Carmona, D. (eds). (Tarragona: Intercultural Studies Group). http://isg.urv.es date accessed 21 November 2014.

Paletta, A. 2012. "Lost in Translation, Found in Subtitles". *The Wall Street Journal*, October 4 2012. http://online.wsj.com date accessed 4 October 2012.

Paulos, E. 2013. "The Rise of the Expert Amateur: DIY Culture and the Evolution of Computer Science", *ASPLOS*, pp. 153–154.

Pavesi, M. 2008. "Spoken Language in Film Dubbing: Target Language Norms, Interference and Translational routines". In Chiaro, D., Heiss C. and Bucaria, C. (eds) *Between Text and Image: Updating Research in Screen Translation.* (Amsterdam & Philadelphia: John Benjamins), pp. 79–100.

Pavesi, M. 2005. *La traduzione filmica. Aspetti del parlato doppiato dall'inglese all'italiano.* (Roma: Carocci).

Pedersen, J. 2011. *Subtitling Norms for Television: an Exploration Focusing on Extralinguistic Cultural References.* (Amsterdam: John Benjamins).

Perego, E. 2010. "La sottotitolazione sperimentale degli *anime* e le norme contravvenute: cosa ci dicono i tracciati oculari". In *Dubbing cartoonia: Mediazione interculturale e funzione didattica nel processo di traduzione dei cartoni animati*, De Rosa, G. L. (ed.), pp. 47–58. (Napoli: Loffredo Editore).

Perego, E. 2007. *La traduzione audiovisiva.* (Roma: Carocci Editore).

DOI: 10.1057/9781137470379.0012

Pérez-González, L. 2013. "Amateur Subtitling as Immaterial Labour in Digital Media Culture: an Emerging Paradigm of Civic Engagement". *Convergence: The International Journal of Research into New Media Technologies*,19 (2), pp. 157–175.

Pérez González, L. 2007. "Intervention in New Amateur Subtitling Cultures: a Multimodal Account", *Linguistica Antverpiensia 6*, pp. 67–80.

Pérez González, L. 2006. "Fansubbing Anime: Insights into the 'Butterfly Effect' of Globalisation on Audiovisual Translation", *Perspectives: Studies in Translatology,* 14(4), pp. 260–277.

Pérez-González, L and Susam-Saraeva, S. 2012, "Non-professionals Translating and Interpreting. Participatory and Engaged Perspectives", *The Translator*, 18(2), pp. 149–165.

Pym, A. et al. 2012. "The Status of the Translation Profession in the European Union", *The European Commission's Directorate-General for Translation*. http://isg.urv.es date accessed 01 November 2013.

Pym, A., Shlesinger, M. and Simeoni, D. (eds). 2008. *Beyond Descriptive Translation Studies: Investigations in Homage to Gideon Toury*. (Amsterdam, Netherlands: John Benjamins).

Raffaelli, S. 1994. "Il parlato cinematografico e televisivo". In Serianni, L. and Trifone, P. (eds) *Storia della lingua italiana. Vol. II. Scritto e parlato*. (Torino: Enaudi), pp. 271–290.

Rembert-Lang, L. D. 2010. "Reinforcing the Tower of Babel: The Impact of Copyright Law on Fansubbing", *Intellectual Property Brief,* 2(2), pp. 21–33.

Rossi, F. 2002. "Il dialogo nel parlato filmico". In Bazzanella, C. (ed.), *Sul dialogo. Contesti e forme di interazione verbale*. (Milano: Guerini), pp. 161–175.

Rossi, F. 1999. "Realismo dialettale, ibridismo italiano-dialetto, espressionismo regionalizzato: Tre modelli linguistici del cinema italiano", *Proceedings of the SILFI Conference, Catania*.

Scandura, G. L. 2004. "Sex, Lies and TV: Censorship and Subtitling", *Meta: Translators' Journal,* 49(1), 125–134. www.erudit.org/revue/meta/2004/v49/n1/009028ar.pdf. Accessed 1 November 2014.

Schleiermacher, F. 1813. "On the Different Methods of Translating". Berlin.

Scholz, T. 2013. (ed.). *Digital Labour: the Internet as Playground and Factory*. (New York: Routledge).

DOI: 10.1057/9781137470379.0012

Scholz, T. 2008. "Market Ideology and the Myths of Web 2.0", *First Monday*, 13(3). www.uic.edu/htbin/cgiwrap/bin/ojs/index.php/fm/article/viewArticle/2138/1945 date accessed 13 August 2014.

Sevignani, S. and Fuchs, C. 2013. "What Is Digital Labour? What Is Digital Work? What's Their Difference? And Why Do These Questions Matter for Understanding Social Media?", *TripleC*, 11(2), pp. 237–293.

Sokoli, S. 2011." Subtitling Norms in Greece and Spain. A comparative Descriptive Study on Film Subtitle Omission and Distribution", *Academia.Edu PhD thesis*. www.academia.edu date accessed 25 September 2012.

Sperber, D. andWilson, D. 1995. *Relevance: Communication and Cognition. Second Edition.*

(Oxford: Blackwell).

Surowiecki, J. 2005. *The Wisdom of Crowds*. (New York: Anchor Books).

Sützl, W., Stalder, F., Maier, R. & Hug T. 2012. (eds) *Media, Knowledge, and Education: Cultures and Ethics of Sharing.* (Innsbruck: Innsbruck University Press).

Toffler, A. and Toffler, H. 1980. *The Third Wave*. (London: Pan Books).

Toury, G. 1995. *Descriptive Translation Studies and Beyond.* (Amsterdam, Netherlands: John Benjamins).

Toury, G. 1980. *In Search of a Theory of Translation.* (Tel Aviv: The Porter Institute for Poetics and Semiotics, Tel Aviv University).

Tveit, J. E. 2009. "Dubbing vs. Subtitling: Old Battleground Revisited". In Díaz-Cintas, J. and Anderman, G. (eds) *Audiovisual Translation, Language Transfer on Screen.* (London: Palgrave Macmillan), pp. 85–96.

Vellar, A. 2011. " 'Lost' (and Found) in Transculturation. The Italian Networked Collectivism of US TV Series and Fansubbing Performances". In Colombo, F. and Fortunati, L. (eds) *Broadband Society and Generational Changes.* (Oxford: Peter Lang), pp. 1–14.

Venuti, L. 2008. *The Translator's Invisibility: A History of Translation.* (London and New York: Routledge).

Vermeer, H. 1989. "Skopos and Translation Commission in Translational Activity". In Venuti, L. *The Translation Studies Reader.* (London: Routledge).

DOI: 10.1057/9781137470379.0012

Index

DOI: 10.1057/9781137470379.0013

DOI: 10.1057/9781137470379.0013

GPSR Compliance
The European Union's (EU) General Product Safety Regulation (GPSR) is a set
of rules that requires consumer products to be safe and our obligations to
ensure this.

If you have any concerns about our products, you can contact us on

ProductSafety@springernature.com

In case Publisher is established outside the EU, the EU authorized
representative is:

Springer Nature Customer Service Center GmbH
Europaplatz 3
69115 Heidelberg, Germany